PROGRESS

PROGRESS

Answers and solutions for a more progressive Bahamas

BY

JULIAN PEDICAN

iUniverse, Inc.
Bloomington

Thank you for supporting me by purchasing this book and taking the time out to read it, this book has become a landmark in my life; I'm happy and very thankful that you are giving me the opportunity to share my views and ideas with you. Do everything with love peace and respect, and may god bless you and yours.

Yours truly

Julian Pedican

PROGRESS
Answers and Solutions for a more Progressive Bahamas

Copyright © 2011 by Mr. Julian Pedican.

All rights reserved. No part of this book may be used or reproduced by any means, graphic, electronic, or mechanical, including photocopying, recording, taping or by any information storage retrieval system without the written permission of the publisher except in the case of brief quotations embodied in critical articles and reviews.

Mr. Julian F. Pedican
P.O.BOX # SB- 50804
NASSAU,BAHAMAS
email: sirjulianss@hotmail.com

iUniverse books may be ordered through booksellers or by contacting:

iUniverse
1663 Liberty Drive
Bloomington, IN 47403
www.iuniverse.com
1-800-Authors (1-800-288-4677)

Because of the dynamic nature of the Internet, any web addresses or links contained in this book may have changed since publication and may no longer be valid. The views expressed in this work are solely those of the author and do not necessarily reflect the views of the publisher, and the publisher hereby disclaims any responsibility for them.

Any people depicted in stock imagery provided by Thinkstock are models, and such images are being used for illustrative purposes only.
Certain stock imagery © Thinkstock.

ISBN: 978-1-4620-7357-3 (sc)
ISBN: 978-1-4620-7358-0 (hc)
ISBN: 978-1-4620-7359-7 (ebk)

Printed in the United States of America

iUniverse rev. date: 12/21/2011

ACKNOWLEDGMENTS

First, I would like to thank my heavenly father for loving us all unconditionally, and my Lord and savior Jesus Christ, and the Holy Spirit, because all of my Knowledge and wisdom comes from our Lord God and it is he who gave me the abilities to see things other people can't see, and answers that people can't find, for without my God I would be nothing.

DEDICATIONS

This book is dedicated to my mother Ms. Marjorie Sarah Pedican, born March 12, 1951 in Green Turtle Cay Abaco to February 11, 2004. My mother was a kind loving and a very generous woman, who never thought twice about giving someone her last, she was well loved and respected by all whom she came into contact with, her smile and personality was like the sun, bright warm and captivating. That is something you can always depend on when it comes to Marjorie Pedican, I can't remember once hearing her say something bad about anyone because it was always love with her, she was also an excellent cook, everybody loved her food. May your soul rest in love and peace mom until our Lord and Savior returns; see (Proverbs 31:10-31)

And to my brother Mr. Garvin M. Pedican Sr., he was just like our mother loved and respected and was a cool person to be around. Gone to soon, may your soul rest in love and peace my brother until our Lord and Savior returns.

CONTENTS

INTRODUCTION

INCOME TAX & COMPANY TAX...................................... 1

FOOD & OVER THE COUNTER PRESCRIPTION

DRUGS.. 20

FARMING & FISHING INDUSTRIES.............................. 25

RULES FOR M.P'S & CORRUPTION............................... 33

SOLUTIONS FOR THE NUMBER RACKET..................... 40

REGULATIONS FOR NEW & USED CARS DEALERS   47

LABOR BOARD & MINUMUM WAGE.......................... 51

THE POLICE FORCE & INTELLIGENCE AGENCIES........ 54

CUBA & ANDROS... 65

NEW FORMS OF CLEAN ENERGY................................. 77

RECYCLING... 80

THE CHURCH... 83

LAWS THAT NEED TO CHANGE..................................... 90

THE ECONOMY OF BAHAMAS....................................... 95

THE NEW AIRPORT & HOSPITAL...............................	114
REGULATIONS FOR LAWYERS, DOCTORS, BANKERS, CONTRACTORS & INSURANCE CO.............	119
THE ILLEGAL IMMIGRANT PROBLEM.........................	124
RESPECTS...	125
MEN, WOMEN, & KIDS IN SOCIETY...........................	130
HONORING GREAT BAHAMIEN MEN & WOMEN...	134
WORKING TOGETHER FOR A BETTER BAHAMAS.......	139
INTEGRITY..	143
MONEY..	146
THE BAHAMAS LOTTERY..	151
PROGRESS...	154

INCOME TAX

There is some kind of tax in every county in the entire world, but I believe income tax is the most necessary form of taxation today, it is one of the main ways the government can replenish its cash reserves. Many prominent countries use this type of taxation which is noted as a progressive tax including the United States of America, Canada, the United Kingdom, Demark, Japan, Australia, The Czech Republic, Cuba, China, Israel, Austria, Belgium, Finland, France, Germany, Greece, Hungary, Iceland, Ireland, Italy, South Korea, Luxembourg, Mexico, Netherlands, New Zealand, Norway, Poland, Portugal, Slovakia, Spain, Sweden, Switzerland and Turkey. These are some of the biggest and most powerful countries in world that use this method of taxation.

In 1913 the United States congressional leader implemented a national income tax so that individuals especially the rich can contribute to their economy. We need an income and company tax system designed just for the Bahamas. All of these countries use a percentage system from 1% to 60% based on the individual gross income. Looking at the size of our county and the amount of people which has been estimated at 350,000; this tax system must be the right fit for Bahamians and also persons who are not Bahamians but have possessed work permits.

What I'm going to do is break the tax system down in a simple form for you. I know you might be thinking that we don't need any new type of taxation system or new taxes because we are being taxed too much already.

I will address that specific issue for you after I give you the formula and then the answer to the formula.

The last government indicated that there are three hundred and fifty thousand Bahamians in the Bahamas, so let's just say that there are one hundred and fifty thousand Bahamians that are working in the county and the other two hundred thousand people are babies, teenagers and older people. As you can see I'm using the smaller amount, so let's break this one hundred and fifty thousand working people into fifteen groups, which would be ten thousand people in each group. And we will be using 3.85% out of the 1% to 60% that the large counties are using. Group one makes $200 per week, group two makes $250, group three makes $300, group four makes $350, group five makes $400, group six makes $450, group seven makes $500, group eight $550, group nine $600, group ten $650, group eleven $700, group twelve $750, group thirteen $800, group fourteen $850 and group fifteen $900. All of these fifteen different groups reflect the weekly pay roll of Bahamians that are working in the Bahamas. Here is the formula:

$200x 52wks = $10,400 -3.85% = $400 x 10,000 = $4,000,000.

$250 x 52wks = $13,000 -3.85% = $500 x 10,000 = $5,000,000.

$300 x 52wks = $15,600 -3.85% = $600 x 10,000 = $6,000,000.

$350 x 52wks = $18,200 -3.85% = $700 x 10,000 = $7,000,000.

$400 x 52wks = $20,800 - 3.85% = $800 x 10,000 = $8,000,000.

$450 x 52wks = $23,400 - 3.85% = $900 x 10,000 = $9,000,000.

$500 x 52wks = $26,000 - 3.85% = $1000 x 10,000 = $10,000,000.

$550 x 52wks = $28,600 - 3.85% = $1100 x 10,000 = $11,000,000.

$600 x 52wks = $31,200 - 3.85% = $1200 x 10,000 = $12,000,000.

$650 x 52wks = $33,800 - 3.85% = $1300 x 10,000 = $13,000,000.

$700 x 52wks = $36,400 - 3.85% = $1400 x 10,000 = $14,000,000.

$750 x 52wks = $39,000 - 3.85% = $1500 x 10,000 = $15,000,000.

$800 x 52wks = $41,600 - 3.85% = $1600 x 10,000 = $16,000,000.

$850 x 52wks = $44,200 - 3.85% = $1700 x 10,000 = $17,000,000.

$900 x 52wks = $46,800 - 3.85% = $1800 x 10,000 = $18,000,000.

The total amount $165,000,000.

That's the amount that I came up with; now this is just a rough number I came up with using basic math, so think about what the government can do with this type of money every year, and there will be more than one hundred and sixty five million dollars coming in to the treasury a year because there are more than one hundred and fifty thousand people working in the Bahamas.

We can do the percentage system another way, what if the

3.85 % is not enough, for some people we can do 5% from $500 up to $750 per week and $751 and up to $1,000 would be 7% weekly and 10% from $1001 and up, that will work even better. If the government can get this kind of money each year from income tax that would be excellent, and when the population grows to five hundred thousand then we take a look at taking the percentage up a little more if it is needed.

Now the way I see how we can go about collecting this income tax is by dividing it over a fifty two week span and then the employer can deduct it from the weekly pay of the employees, then the employer can send the tax in at the end of the month or three months just like N.I.B but more effective than N.I.B in collecting these taxes. You might say that this tax system is the same as the U.S, taking a percentage out of individual's weekly pay. Yes it is but this is the simplest and the best way to do this tax system, and the percentage is not 20 to 50 percent like it is in the U.S, its 3.85% to 5% to 7% and 10%. We would not ask for a percentage of all your income that comes into your household like commissions and bonuses but if you have two jobs then you will pay five or seven or ten percent tax from each job.

And everybody must pay income tax, from the Prime Minster going down the line to the person who cleans your yard or your house or your pool. The person who fixes your car and even the lunch ladies who are in the parking lot at your work place to the people who are here on work permits from barbers to hair dressers, police men, lawyers, doctors, accountants, I mean from the top to the bottom of this economy.

The CEO's of companies that do not pay income and company taxes would be charged with not paying government taxes and the owner or owners will be arrested and fined from $50,000 and up, and will be facing jail time. The government must have tough laws behind the tax systems because if not, the employer will take it as a joke and paying taxes is not a joking matter.

It's important that the government and the people of the Bahamas start using this form of taxation so by the time the population grows to five or six hundred thousand they will be used to paying income tax and already adjusted to this system.

This progressive income tax system should have been done a long time ago in this country but when we look at it from the late 70s to the end of the 80s the economy was doing well with the off shore banking, construction and tourism and foreign investors. Money was flowing into the county from all over the world, then the 90s came around and the county was still on an upswing until September, 11 2001. That was one of the worst days in U.S. history, the attack on the country and the economy itself. The attacks on the world trade center in New York and the Pentagon in Washington D.C were horrendous and it could have been worst as they almost attacked the White House. This attack caused a slowdown in almost every sector including, tourism and construction. This resulted in a spending slowdown in the Bahamas. Now may God forbid that type of attack will never happen again? Our economy went on a slow down because of 9/11, and the Bahamas government slowed down its spending because the treasury was not getting money like it was before, things got tight and it took years after that for the Bahamas economy to start looking up.

Whatever happens in the U.S. economy it takes a toll on the Bahamas economy. We are too, and I want to emphasize this, we are too dependent on the United States. It is almost like we are a 38 year old man still drinking milk from the baby bottle or from his mother.

Tourism is our number one industry that brings in money into the treasury, but when there is a problem in the U.S. we feel the problem here in the Bahamas, like when Americans started losing their jobs and homes in the U.S. they reduced their vacation travel, many putting off travel for their families to the Bahamas. This year, when gas prices went up sky high it also meant many boaters would no longer be taking their boats to the Bahamas three or four times a year. If five middle class Americans were on that boat then that means thousands of dollars less is being spent between hotel, food, drinks and buying other things. This shows you how whatever happens in the U.S. affects us in the Bahamas.

But if we had a progressive income tax in this country that means that the treasury would see about $165,000,000 dollars at least every year being put into the treasury and into a C.D. account. This amount is just tax on salaries and there is still more to come with the company taxes and other taxes.

I would like to see this system in place but I can't be upset about not having a progressive income tax system in the Bahamas, because the U.S. did not start their income tax system until 1913 and they had been independent for two hundred and twenty seven years. That means that is only ninety seven years ago, and they have billions or trillions of dollars at their disposal. So think about it if we were doing this income tax system from the late 70's until now we would have at least between ten to twenty billion dollars at our disposal.

This kind of liquid cash in our treasury would do our county well and reduce us from depending so much on other countries and we can pay for what we want. We have now in our treasury over one point five billion dollars. I have rounded off that figure because I heard the Prime Minster say on T.V that there is three hundred million over here and seven hundred million over there and another three hundred million over there in foreign currency cash reserves.

Now I know that a lot of Bahamian people would say that, I don't want no more money coming out of my paycheck N.I.B is enough. Before I say that these people are selfish and they don't care about their county, I'll say this N.I.B is not for the government, this tax is for the Bahamian people even though the government borrows from it time from to time. This fund is sometimes used when the government's liquid cash reserves are not enough. When you put money into N.I.B. you will get back from N.I.B; like when you have a broken leg or when you are having a baby or when you are retired at about sixty or sixty five years of age and eligible to receive monthly payments. Let me point something out about Bahamians, they do not like to give, not all Bahamians, but the majority of them I believe do not like to give. JESUS said in the book of Luke 6:38 "Give, and it shall be given unto you; good measure, pressed down, and shaken together, and running over, shall men give into your bosom. For with the same measure that ye meter with it shall be measured to you again". But they would say that I can't afford it, we all can afford it, and we all can give even if just a little, we (ALL) can give.

PROGRESS

When a man says he cannot give any more money out of his pocket, sometimes it is because he must have money for his wife and his sweetheart and sometimes these men will have two sweethearts, three kids with his wife and one or two with the sweetheart, (this is for who the cap fits). In addition to that some men must have money to buy drinks on the weekend, and must pay for his sweetheart's hairdo and nails to be fixed so that she would look good for some other guy because that's not his wife and she making herself look good so that other men would want her. Men's spending habits are many times on sweet hearting, drinking and smoking and partying. Some of them will spend on drinking about $75 to $90 dollars a week. If you multiply that by fifty two weeks that means it will be between $3,900 and $4,680 dollars a year. Those who smoke will spend on one pack of smokes about $6.00 dollars. Let's say one pack a week multiplied by fifty two weeks that's $312.00 dollars or more. This is not to mention the money spent on the sweethearts. When you round it all off, taking into account her hair and nails and clothes and putting money in her pocket, that could be more than $5,000 dollars a year, give or take a few dollars. If you add all these unnecessary expenses it will amount to more than $10,000 a year. Some men will do all three of these things while some men will do two, and some only one and some men do none at all.

The ones who do so give away a lot of money in one year, between five and ten thousand dollars for bad habits. These men who don't like this idea of income tax feel like they can't give half of the five or ten thousand dollars a year in bad habits to the government for income tax for the county. This is wrong and if they can waste money on bad habits they can help their country by putting this money to good use.

Women would sometimes say they can't give no more money to the government because they have a lot of bills, bills like rent, car payments and some have three kids and some have four or five kids plus light bills, water bills, food for the house and more. What surprises me is that these same women would have a new car, the latest clothes and have fifty or sixty pairs of shoes that they do not wear. They also have Gucci and Donnie and Burke bags that cost eight and nine hundred dollars each and let's not forget the Cartier and David Yurman jewelry and all the latest things. I know because I have seven sisters, so there is no question that I know. Some women would say that their man bought these things for them. That's not my business if that is the case. Some women would say I buy these things for myself, as an independent woman, but that just proves my point that you can't give 3.85% to 5% to7% or up to 10% of your yearly income to the government for income tax. For the women who say their man bought these things for them, just take the money and put some of it towards the bill so that you can pay your income tax out of your own pay.

I'm not saying that you can't have these things and that you can't enjoy the fruits of your labor but we the country, the people and the government needs you to give a little of your income so we can do a lot of other things for the country and its people or in other words (YOU) and I believe that not asking too much.

There are some political parties that don't want to tell you that we need this type of tax system because they think it will cause them not to win the election and that is not fair to you or to the country.

The reason why we need this income tax system, besides the fact that the government needs a consistent flow of money each year and that it is the right thing to do, it is also because other large and rich counties are doing it and they seem to be able to do good by the people with jobs health care and building up their country. Don't you want the same things for your country?

SMALL BUSINESS & COMPANY TAX

I think I have an idea of what most of the C.E.O.'s and the bosses of these small businesses in the Bahamas would say about this small business and company tax. I believe they will say that it is not fair that we have to pay company and small business tax to the government because we pay custom duties and stamp tax on all of the goods and products that we bring in to the county already. Why do we need to pay more tax to government? I will answer this question later, but for now let me give you the formula and the then the answer.

In the U.S., companies pay tax to government based on their profit margin, the U.S. government takes a percentage of the company's profits for their treasury, that's why the president of the United States would say on Television that the big companies have too many tax breaks and they are still sending jobs out of county.

I am not suggesting that form of tax system for the Bahamas. I suggest that we use one that is very unique and easy and much better for companies and small business in the Bahamas. It's simple. This tax system is based on the amount of employees the companies have. The dollar amount that we will be using is from ten dollars to one hundred dollars. There are companies that have from one to five thousand employees. Let us say for example a food store chain has about one hundred and ninety employees. This company would then pay $75.00 dollars per person a year which will be $75 x 190 = $14,250 a year in taxes to the government.

For another example let us say this hotel has about five hundred employees, that hotel will have a yearly company tax of $40.00 dollars per person a year so that's $40 x 500 = $20,000 a year in company taxes to the government.

Another example would be a bank chain that has about three thousand employees, the bank will pay a yearly tax of twenty dollars a year per person which would be $20 x 3000 = $60,000. That's $60,000 a year in taxes to the government.

Here is another example, let us say there is a plumbing company that has sixty nine employees, the yearly company tax is ninety five dollars per person a year that's $95 x 69 = $6,555.00 so that's $6,555.00 a year in taxes to the government.

If I have about seven employees, that means that my yearly company taxes to the government will be, 7 x $100 = $700 dollars, that's only $700 dollars a year to the government in small business taxes.

This I believe is the best way to do this because this formula is good for small business, big companies and the government. It is based on the amount of employees that the business has, and not the government taking a large percentage from the company's profits, instead the amount of employees determines what the company pays.

For contrast let us look at it this way, what if the government was to take a percentage of your company profits. If the government were to take 25% of the $80,000 dollars of your companies' profits, your company would be left with $60,000 dollars in profits a year.

By comparison if your company has ten employees including the owner of the company, you would pay in company tax $1,000 ($100 x 10 = 1,000 a year). The difference should now be clear between the percentage based system and paying taxes based on the amount of employees. Even if the percentage

was 5% company taxes would still be more than the employee number based system. I am sure the C.E.O; s and company bosses of these companies would prefer the system that is based upon number of employees rather than a percentage of profits.

If we were to use this system and if there are one hundred and fifty thousand people working in the county, in small businesses and larger companies, if every company and small business pays fifty dollars in taxes for each person working for that business or company that would be around seven million five hundred thousand dollars a year in taxes. Every little bit counts. For the construction companies that hire based on the size of job and how long the job will run for, the government collection agency will determine what the company would pay.

I would propose that the only people that would be exempted from this income tax system would be young people from age 18 to 22 so that if they want to go to college after high school they can use the money that they have worked for to pay for their books and school fees. For the people who have diplomatic status in country, no one else from the Prime Minister down to the people who clean the roads would be exempt. People with work permits and the bosses and C.E.O'S who run the companies even if they don't take home a paycheck will still have to contribute. The bosses and the C.E.O'S are given an amount to pay based upon whatever their highest paid employee is making. They would pay more than that amount.

Churches and the people who work in the churches should also pay company and income taxes because many church leaders are running their churches like a business and not like the house of God. Of course that is my opinion but I will leave it up to government to make that decision.

Using the words of JESUS, he said in Matt 22:19-20-21; "show me the tribute money, (20) whose is the image and superscription? (21) They say unto him, Caesar's. Then say he unto them Render therefore unto Caesar the things which are Caesar's; and unto god the things that are gods".

In the examples used the total of company tax for these five companies would be $101,505. That is only the total for five companies, so think of how many companies and small business there are in the Bahamas that have employees and the amount of taxes that will go into the treasury.

I believe the best way for the government to collect these income, small business and company taxes, is by opening a new branch of government that will work side by side with

N.I.B. to collect taxes. That means more jobs for Bahamians at least one hundred additional persons. In addition many companies will have to hire more employees in their accounts department to deal with the paper work.

Let me share with you why I believe it is so important that we need this type of income and company taxes in the Bahamas. Imagine looking at your children in the face and telling them that you do not care about their future and their children's future, and telling them that it does not matter if they get robbed or if they eat today or not, because you can't give 3.85%, 5%, 7% or up to 10% of your yearly pay to the government as income tax. You would not tell them that because you want the best for your children and you want them to have the best in life. That is what this income and company taxes is all about, and that's why we should be happy to pay this type of tax, so we can have a better Bahamas and a better life for Bahamians. This will also mean more development and building projects like the new hospital and new airports in the Family Islands. The more building projects means more jobs in the county and the government can pay for better advertisement and promotions in other counties like Europe, U.K., Japan, Italy and the other counties in the world.

This will boost tourism and bring millions of people and investors into our county, who will spend hundreds of millions of dollars with us. The first rule of business is you must spend money in order to make money. I understand this clearly, the importance of spending money on advertising, product development, and good people, staff who know how to deal with people from all walks of life. We need to be able to and advertise to the world who we are and what we are about. You can sit down and think of the things the Bahamas government can do with the five to six hundred million dollars a year that comes in from customs duties, income and company taxes and tourism. One of these benefits would be cutting the duty on food that comes in to the country at by least 20%; so people in the country can eat much better because food is a necessity and it is the governments duty to make sure that the people are able to afford the necessities in life.

The additional company and income taxes will just add to that amount that goes into the treasury. Between income and company taxes the estimated amount that I came up with is almost two hundred million dollars a year, to go into the treasury or government savings for hard times or major nationwide disaster. In the Bahamas, the middle class and the poor should know what I'm talking about when I refer to hard times as the old folks used to say, "You better save some for a rainy day". That C.D. account is for rainy days to come. Remember the story in the bible in the book of GENESIS.41: about the seven years of plenty and seven years of famine. Let's use the wisdom and Knowledge that God has given some of us, let us show them better than we can tell them, I'm talking to the leaders and the Bahamian people.

When a government CD savings account is set up it should be stipulated that the only way that the government can unlock this C.D. account is an act of parliament, with 90% of parliament being required to approve the opening of this C.D. account instead of the simple majority. It should be further stipulated that not even the Prime Minister can unlock this account by himself; he must have 90% of parliament with him, and three, it should be no provision for borrowing from or against it.

In the coming chapters I will show you all of the good things that this income and company tax can do for us in this country and I will show you how we can get more money into the treasury from other places so that the government can do more good things for us Bahamians. And if this income and company tax system is too much for you to digest then look at it this way that you are making your country and economy strong by paying taxes to the government. If we do

PROGRESS

this it means less dependence on other countries and more depending on ourselves. This will be the beginning of a wonderful Bahamas to come, now that's progress, so read on and enjoy.

FOOD & PRESCRIPTION DRUGS

The cost of food has climbed to its highest in years mainly because of high oil prices. The rising price of oil is sending the price of everything up, some of those things are things we do not need and some we can live without, but food is something that we cannot live without. Let's say the percentage of duty on food is about 45%, if the government were to cut the duty down to 27% that would be good for the poor and the middle class alike. It is not that the government would be losing all the duty on food, just a percentage of it. Let's say the government takes in one hundred million dollars a year in duties from food products and then the duty was cut to 27%, from 45%. Some people would say that's more than half and that is too much duty to take off but my point of emphasis is to put more food into the Bahamian household, and not to let them starve.

That will still leave about 73 million dollars a year from 100 million dollars. The more that people can afford the more they will spend. Some bread basket items like bread, flower, rice, and grits are duty free and some canned goods are only 10%. The question I must ask is, why are some of the bread basket items are so high in priced? I believe it is not right to have these items being sold at high prices. Some people would say how can we do this? My response is what about the money from the treasury? What about the 73 million dollars a year.

The idea in chapter one is that the people give, and then the government gives back, they give to the government in income tax and then the government cuts the duties on food and other things. Cutting the duty on food is the best place to start, as the government is not losing the whole one hundred million, just twenty seven million of the one hundred million. One of the government mandates is to make it better for the people of the Bahamas. Let me show you what some of the prices in the stores are like.

1 gallon of milk$8.59, 1 gallon orange juice $7.49, cheese single of 24 in the pack $7.19, eggs $3.69 an up, rice for a 10lb bag, $8.99, cooking oil $4.89, butter $5.95, bread $3.59. I remember when bread was$1.19, and a gallon of milk was $ 4.89 and I am sure that many of you remember those days also.

Looking at the cleaning products, Ariel 5lb $7.99, small Pine Sol $4.89, box of Tide$11.59, tooth paste starts at $3.45, mouthwash $7.29 and tooth brushes $3.85.

Let us take a look at some baby products, Pedialight $8.55 for 1qt, one baby bottle $3.99, baby diapers pack of 14 starts at $10.99, baby wipes $5.29, Enfamil 12oz $17.89 and the 25oz $16.99, baby food in the jar $1.19 each.

When you go in the food stores you will see just what I am talking about. If I was the leader of this county this would be one of the first changes I would make.

OVER THE COUNTER AND PRESCRIPTION DRUGS

At the same time the government addresses the food it should do the same for prescription and over the counter drugs. I remember when I was sick, I went to the private doctor and I had to wait a very long time, by the time I got to see the doctor I went in and sat down and was waiting another 10 to 15 minutes, then the doctor came in and asked some questions and then he examined me, in five to ten minutes he was finished and I was out of his office. He wrote me a prescription for some medication, and I looked at the prescription and because of his bad hand writing I wasn't able to make out what was on the paper so I paid $75 dollars for the doctor visit, then I went and fulfilled the prescription for $35 dollars, only to find out it was the same medication I had at home already, an over the counter medication. I was angry or as we would say in the Bahamas I was hot, (hot as in mad) because I had I spent $110 dollar for nothing. There are a lot of people that can't afford to see a private doctor every time something happens, and that is fine, once they can buy their medication that they need in an affordable manner. It is critical that persons would be able to afford their medication.

It's very import that people can afford their medication so that they can stay healthy; this is good for old folk and people with long term sicknesses. If the government gets $80 million dollars a year from prescription drugs, and they cut some of the duties off, let say 20% off prescription drugs that still leaves $64 million dollars a year coming in to the treasury a year. It could be done, so let me show you some of the prices of the over the counter drugs in the stores.

Robitussin $5.19, Tylenol $8.39, Theraflu $6.79, Advil $7.89, Aleve $7.59, Buckley $6.49, Nyquil $14.55 and Dimetapp $6.75. If someone said that these prices are not high that means that they can afford them with no problem. If these are the prices for over the counter medications imagine the prices of the prescription drugs. We need lower priced drugs in order to keep the people of the Bahamas healthy, so they can be more productive.

FARMING & FISHING INDUSTRIES

If someone were to rate our farming industry from 1 to 10 we would be rated no higher than a 1 ½, perhaps not even that. I say this because the farming industry in Bahamas is not where it could be, it is hard to even call it a farming industry. At this point and until we do better I would say that we are allowed to grow some fruits and vegetable for the country, this is insulting to the hard working men and women who get up at 5am every morning and work the fields, I'm simply recognizing that we are not doing enough.

Let me say this to the men and women who are working on the farms, thank you so much for your hard work and dedication to the farming industry. The reason why I said that we are allowed to farm is because it seems like the government has only allowed Bahamians to farm to keep them quiet. Some would say the government has nothing to do with the farmers and that is exactly my point.

The government has no broad, integrated program or plan for the farming industry; it is like the farmers are on their own. I am not saying the government does absolutely nothing, the government gives a little here and there but that is not enough. Across the Bahamas from Andros, Abaco, Eleuthera, Mayaguana, Acklins & Crooked Island, San Salvador, Rum cay, Great Inagua, Long Island, and Grand Bahama there are millions of acres of crown land doing nothing. You might ask what can the government do about this. Here is what I think the government should do. The government should launch a

$250 million dollar program for the farming industry. You might ask where is the money coming from and why should the government give $250 million dollars to the farming industry. The money will have to come from the public treasury because this is one industry that we need to be developed so we can move toward being independent. The farming industry is the most important industry in the world. I am sure you would know this is a great need and as a country we need to take part in this world wide industry for our own sake.

This $250 million dollars should be divided into different amounts; $65 million dollars should be spent on farming equipment, like for land clearing, fencing, buildings, animals, moving equipment, and to build barns for chickens, cows, pigs, turkeys, sheep and horses. These funds would also be used for the chickens to lay eggs, for cows to give hundred of gallons of fresh milk, for the pigs to have piglets, sheep and horses. The barns should be built on most of the family islands. I believe $60 million dollars should be spent on buying live stock from farms and for testing of the animals and for seeds for the crops. Twenty million dollars should be spent for packing and saving livestock and other products in freezer warehouses. Part of this should also be spent on slaughter houses for the live stock.

We should also provide $10 million dollars for a medical team to take care of all the live stock, a mobile team that moves from island to island and a team of veterinarians, their assistants and their helpers, and $10 million dollars to send young Bahamians to school to become veterinarians. We should also send Bahamians off to school who would specialize in agriculture and farming. I also believe that $85 million should be allocated on other services that go along with farming and raising animals and crops.

All of the land needed, should be donated by the government. The focus of development should be on products that are used in everyday life, things that people use to cook with in

their homes and in the Caribbean life like, wheat ,corn, banana, tomatoes, lettuce, carrots, green pepper, celery, cabbage, potatoes, onions, oranges, limes, plantains, cantaloupes, watermelon, spinach, peas, lemons and broccoli.

We have many farmers who can do the work because they have dedicated their lives to the farming industry. If a farmer is growing tomatoes, then that farmer should be given more acres of land so that they can increase the output of product. Also if a farmer is growing lettuce then that farmer should be given more acres of land so he can increase the amount of products produced. Farmers who are growing live stock should be given land and equipment so they can produce more livestock. Once this is done a big campaign can be launched to promote agriculture which would then lead to more jobs for the Bahamian people. If we produce our own products it would mean less dependency on other countries. As we continue with agricultural development, the more input into farming means more output and as output expands the time will come when it will be time to export which will mean a big bonus for the Bahamas and for the people of the Bahamas.

Our first obligation is to establish and grow this industry and once we are able to feed ourselves we can begin exporting things link beef, pork, lamb, chicken, turkey, fresh fruit and vegetables. Now of course we must be cleared and certified to export these products.

If we as a people and a country start this campaign, now do you know what we can do in five years, we can start feeding our own population and in seven to ten years we can be exporting. I will not go as far as to say that this campaign would be easy to do, but we can do it with good planning hard work and good hard working people. We can do it by educating Bahamians and setting goals for this industry, and I know we can do this because our fore fathers did it for hundreds of years for their white masters, so why can't we do it for ourselves and our children?

Do you know in the country of Chile one of their biggest industries is farming and they export millions and millions of dollars of fruits and vegetables a year. Chile is a fairly large country and even though we are a smaller country, if we were doing this a long time ago we would have been one of the main exporters of meats and fruits and vegetables in the Caribbean.

The only thing I can say to you is, we as a people and country must, and I say must take on this responsibility so we can safe guard our children's future because the world population is not getting any smaller it is only growing. This growth means more demand for food and meats, so for us to say that we do not need to spend hundreds of millions of dollars on farming is ludicrous. God gave us the sun, the rain and the land, let us be smart and use it, and when we start this campaign the rest of the Caribbean will follow. Before we concentrate on other countries in the Caribbean however, we need to fix our own country first, because I am more concerned about the Bahamas.

The Bahamas is going to be in big trouble if we do not start doing the right things now, by the people, for the country and the government. Please take heed to this book and its contents for your sake, my sake and our kid's sake.

FISHING INDUSTRY

The fishing industry has long been a part of our country and the economy, and fisher men sell millions and millions of dollars of fish, conch, and lobster in one year. It is safe to say that the fishing industry is not only a big part of our country but a big part of the economy, and we all must give thanks to God for all that he has given us in this little country.

In spite of our level of success there are a few things we need to do to protect this industry such as regulating the amount of conch that is exported out of the country. Conch should be a Bahamian thing that you can only get in the Bahamas. I believe that for the most part and you should have a license to export a large amount of conch, because Bahamians consume a large amount of conch as it is now. I believe that as much as possible we should keep conch as a Bahamian thing for Bahamians and our visitors.

(2) We need to take a long break from the Nassau grouper so the fish can replenish itself, something like a five year break, because there are a lot of other fishes that can replace the Nassau grouper like the yellow fin grouper, the red grouper, and red hind grouper, coney grouper, grey grouper, black grouper, scamp grouper. There are also a variety of snapper fish like hog snapper, lane snapper, cub era snapper, gray mangrove snapper, mutton snapper, hogfish snapper, red snapper, school master snapper and yellow tail snapper. In addition to snappers there are about ten

types of jack fish, most of these fishes can be filleted and cooked just like the Nassau groper. Some of these alternative fish taste much better than the Nassau groper and I know because I am a fish lover. You can ask any fishermen or fish lover and I am sure they will say the same thing.

(3) The small under size fish that the fishermen sell on the dock and in restaurants around town should be against the law, just like we do with the under sized lobster we should do with the under size fish.

(4) The government should make it mandatory that there be a national marine park in all of the large islands, and we need to make more reefs, like sinking some old boats, particularly the big ones because the boats become like reefs after a short time and the reefs are where most of the marine life starts.

(5) There should be stiffer fines for illegal fishing and dumping in the waters of the Bahamas. If a fuel tanker has an oil spill this can have a severe impact on our marine life. There are many fuel and oil tankers that are crossing the Bahamian waters and these vessels should have insurance coverage in the Bahamas in the event that there is an accidental oil spill.

The fishing industry is so fragile and important that if we do not take care of it we will be like a boat up the river without any paddles. To look at it another way, if we take care of the fishing industry, then the industry will take care of our needs. There are many ways we can do this. What needs to be done is the persons in charge of the department of fisheries should have meetings with the fishermen on a regular basis and get all the info that is needed to preserve and protect this industry before it gets too late. Now is the time for this.

RULES FOR M.P'S AND CORRUPTION

I have a question to ask you? Is it written somewhere that both political parties must not work together for common goals for the country? If it is written somewhere the person who wrote it should be banned from being able to write again. If someone only said it, that person should be locked up and charged with the stopping of progress and sentenced to quietness for five years, because just the thought of it is foolishness to me. If it is written in a book somewhere the page or that book should be erased from history. The fact of the matter is that I believe both political parties are lacking in vision and have no clear direction about where the country should be going. They are not working together to create a long term plan for the country and its people, it's like the country is going around in circles, because when a party is in power, whatever that party does in their five year term, in the next five years the next new party comes in and walks all over it.

What I believe should happen is that the leaders of the both parties should gather the best and the brightest people with the best ideas for the country and use them and put them together and create a ten or twenty year plan so that progress can come to the Bahamas and stay for long time. Once the plan is complete both parties can agree and sign off on it, so when the next party comes into power the plan for the

Bahamas is already in place. The only competition would then be for the parties to see which party can achieve these goals first. I believe that is not asking for much and the good part about this is that the parties don't have to sell dreams to the people when it's time for an election. That is what I call working together for a common goal and the common good.

Some years ago two members of parliament from the same party had a fight in the house of parliament. Behaviour such as this from parliamentarians is in no way acceptable. Two things should have been done about them; (1) they should have been automatically fired, (2) they both should have been charged with an offence before the court, but these men are still active in their parties and one is a sitting member of the house of parliament.

(3) I also believe that all the members of Parliament should wear a jacket with the Bahamas seal on the pocket of the jacket. I know this sounds like high school students wearing uniforms, but a lot of government and private businesses wear uniforms, and if making the M.P's wear uniforms will help them to work together on one accord then I'm all for that, perhaps you will agree?

(4) No M.P should be talking when the Prime Minster has the microphone.

(5) If there is a big project in the pipe line and one party is about to leave office that parties leader should get together and talk with the incoming party leader to insure that the project will go ahead as planned when and if the next party comes into power. It would be an excellent thing if both parties would stop unnecessarily criticizing the other party because that party came up with a good plan to improve the lives of Bahamians. Instead they should try to add to the plan and help the plan so that they can move forward with it.

(6) If an M.P is caught up in a scandal or criminal activity that M.P should be penalized by the prime minster and the speaker of the house and if it is a serious matter that M.P should be removed from office.

(7) All the M.P's must be present in the house at all times unless there is a medical reason or the person is out of the country on government business, or he or she has been excused by the P.M or the speaker of the house.

See some people might say that these rules are crazy, but remember these people applied for that particular position or that job, we did not force this job on them.

If they don't obey the rules then how do they expect the young people to obey the rules? Make no mistake about it the young people are watching how members act in the house of parliament. When you apply for a job and get the job it comes with rules whether you like it or not. The people in the house of parliament are not there to help themselves; the government is there to help the people and the country move forward. Let us not forget that they need governing also.

The level of corruption in our country has become so insufferable and so thick you need a chainsaw to cut it. This corruption exists from top to bottom from left to right from front to back in and out and round and round, remember now I didn't call any names or point any fingers at any one person, I'm just telling the Gods truth as it is, because in this country people see it, but they don't see what's going on, and they hear it, but they don't hear what's going on around them, or is it that they don't care at all?

What do you think, let's think about it for second? The corruption level needs to be cut by at least half, it does not matter if we start from bottom or top or right or left the point is we need to start somewhere. You might ask who is going to do this. It's Simple, the people who we put in charge of the country we know that some of them are corrupt too but that is their job and they need to just shut-up and do their job. Don't get me wrong about what I am saying, not every single person in this town or country is corrupt. We both know that it is only some of the people who hold big and small positions that make a difference in this country.

I know corruption and crime will never stop until the coming of my Lord and Savior Jesus Christ. Hear what Jesus has to say about the corruption of men. Matthew 7:17-18 "Even so every good tree brings forth good fruit; but a corrupt tree brings forth evil fruit. A good tree cannot bring forth evil fruit; neither can a corrupt tree bring forth good fruit".

The level of corruption can be reduced a whole lot. Let me say this about the difference between corruption and receiving gifts for doing a good job. In my opinion the difference is if you are doing your job one hundred fifty percent better than the other person who is doing the same job, and the people you are doing the work for or providing the service to are very pleased with you and want to show thanks and appreciation for your good works, I think that is okay as long as you are not a part of the justice system or a part of the government. This is different than when a person is corrupt and that person is doing illegal things for his or her own personal or financial gain and does really care about what others say. In my opinion that is the difference between corruption and receiving gifts of appreciation.

I have another question for you. Do you think that corruption slows down progress? That is a question for you to think about. Listen to this and tell me what you think, in September of 2008 we have a hurricane in the southern parts of the Bahamas and it did a lot of damage and within days after help was on the way down south, some people gave money and some people gave supplies. One particular person who gave one hundred thousand dollars to help with repairs, their name was broadcast all over the news media and in the new papers the next day. The interesting thing about this story is that the whole country knows what he does for a living. I do not know him personally and don't have [any] negative feeling against him or anyone who does this for a living but my job in helping our country to progress is to bring the darkness to the light. The whole country knows what he does for a living and where his money comes from. I am sure it is good that he

helped people in times of need and I applauded him for that, but at the same time he was making himself and his business look good and legal, when the truth of the matter is that his business is not legal, he is breaking the law. Or is he?

He is one of the biggest ones engaged in the numbers game, he has shops all over Nassau and the Bahamas and he makes it known that he is selling numbers and does not care about what the law has to say. Many banks indirectly know what he does and where the money comes from but they don't care because they are making money off of his money. On the other hand if a hardworking man or woman comes in to the bank to deposit ten or fifteen thousand dollars on his or her account they will be questioned and will have to fill out another deposit form, but they don't question the "big" man. It is not only this individual that has this kind of business there are about five or ten others and they are almost as big as this person or bigger, who knows? I could name almost all of them but many of you already know who they are. Remember now this is breaking the law, no one is slowing them down or stopping them because when the police close them down one day they open right back up a few days after. For the record it is not the drug business I am referring to, it is the numbers business. After saying all of that you must agree that they must be paying it forward without a doubt. Corruption is an impediment to progress but i will ask the question again do you think that corruption slows down or stops progress?

THE NUMBER RACKET

The numbers racket has long been a part of the Bahamian society, its roots are so deep in this country it's like a hundred year old oak tree and its roots are hundreds of feet deep in the earth, imagine trying to pull this tree up out of the ground, it's like pulling teeth without pain killers. We may not know exactly how long the number racket has been around in this Bahamas but I can tell you this much, that there is no eradicating or wiping the number racket out. That is a task that is easier said than done. As it stands now the number racket is being played by a large number of people in this country, and many different types of people including people like police officers, government employees, church going people the big man, bankers, lawyer, doctors, poor people, the rich folk and believe it or not, even Jamaicans and Haitians are playing numbers as well. In spite of this guess what? The number racket is still illegal in the Bahamas.

The church and some other people have a big problem with the numbers racket and making it legal, but some church people play the game also and maybe even some of the pastors and some bishops. Yes it might be wrong, but according to biblical law, so is having sweethearts and drinking and bad Language and just like the rest of sins people do each day that the bible warns against. Yet people from all walks of life commit these sins, but it's not my place to say if they are right or wrong or to judge them in playing numbers or gambling, only our Lord and savior Jesus Christ can judge them.

What I'm about to say is for the people who don't want the numbers racket to be made legal. This thought is for you and like it or not it's the truth. God the heavenly father of us all, who created the heavens and the earth, and it is he (God) who marked the sun to rest on the righteous and the unrighteous, and it is he (God) that marked the rain to rain on the just and unjust and it is he (God) who gave his only begotten son our Lord and Savior Jesus Christ to die for our sins, and he also gave us, all of mankind a free will. With this in mind who are you or me to tell a man or woman what to do with their money they have worked so hard for? I'm sure they can't tell you what to do with your money. I mean it's clear as day that if the number racket is legal or illegal they don't care what you have to say they are still going to buy numbers. If you lock them up or not, shout them down or not, they still are going to buy numbers. Think about it for a second what if a man tells you that you can't have sex with your girlfriend or your boyfriend or your sweetheart what would you say? Let me point this fact out first, back in earlier days for as far back as you can remember having sex and not being married and sweet hearting was frowned upon and even now sweet hearting is frowned on and having unmarried sex is a sin. So what would you say to that man or woman who tells you that you can't have sex with your boyfriend or girlfriend or sweetheart? I think I have an idea what some people would say, mind your own business, don't tell me what to do with my life, you don't run my life, don't judge me because only (God) can judge me, I have to answer to (God) for my sins not you so stay out of my business. This is my point exactly, only (God) can judge them for their sins, and you can't tell them how to live their life or what to do with their money they've worked for.

Telling people not to play numbers is the same as telling them not to have sex with their boyfriend or girlfriend or sweetheart because they will do it anyway because it's their life. The only difference in this case is that the numbers racket is against the law.

Let me say this about me playing numbers, I played the numbers two or three times the most in my life and I was only following friends when I was younger. In the present the fact of the matter is I don't play numbers at all, (but it looks like I need to try my hand again at numbers?) and if it was legal, I may or may not play it's because it's a simple matter of moral principle whether I should or not. You might ask the question why I support the number racket. I only support it because if the government makes it legal it will help to sustain our economy by putting more money into the treasury on a monthly basis and creating more jobs, and I'm all for creating a strong economy for us and our children. Let us face it, people are going to play their numbers anyway so if they are going to break the law just to play numbers then the government should make it legal so that the government can organize the whole numbers game and start receiving taxes from the number houses. Aside from this the government cannot afford to lockup half of the country (probably including members of parliament, doctors, lawyers and perhaps even a few judges).

Here is how I think that the government should go about making the numbers racket legal. The government should get all the big number men together and have a meeting with them to let them know what is going to be done, that they are only going to allow them to have three or four large number companies to sell numbers in the country and all the big number men should come together and form the companies. The government should have shares in all three of their companies let's say 25 percent in each company and 23 percent of the shares in each company will be sold on the Bahamas stock market to the public and the number men will divide up the rest of the shares between themselves.

The government will get a percent of all the winnings. If a person wins $800 dollars before that person gets their money a percentage will come out of the winning as tax for the government. For example; from 100 dollar to five thousand dollar there is a 15% tax, so 15% of $800 dollars is $120 dollars for every person that wins. Any amount under five thousand dollars, and from five thousand dollars to twenty thousand dollars it will be 20% and from twenty thousand and up it will be 25%. The number companies will be run just like the big companies with a board of directors and the companies will be regulated by the gaming board who will put offices in the number houses just like the casinos to monitor the winnings and the amount of taxes that should be paid out of the winnings to the government. This monitoring agency will make sure that the number companies are living up to the rules and their mandate set forth by the gaming board. If the number companies don't follow the rules they should have hard penalties assessed and they should have to answer to the authorities.

Let me show you an example of what this can do for the treasury, let us say ten people in one day win six thousand dollars each from playing numbers, that is $60,000 dollars and 15% of that is $9,000 dollar for the treasury in one day and that's only ten players. The number houses have three or more drawings in one day, so think about the amount of people in Nassau and in the country that plays numbers on an everyday basis and imagine the amount of money the treasury would receive. This would certainly be a good thing for our economy.

Think of the things the government can do with the revenue from the number houses. This will teach Bahamians how to work together and by owning shares in a large company they will not continue to think selfishly and that all is for them, but there is enough to go around and around. By making the number racket legal it will automatically create jobs for Bahamians and the money will go round and round in the economy and make a strong foundation just like one made out of cement and steel and not just sand so that our foundation will not wash away.

For too long the number racket has being going on illegally, it is

time to put it in order and make it legal, or "stop" it completely and shut them all down, from the big and the small. If the thought is to shut them down, shutting them down is a very big job for the police, and I truly wish them good luck with a big job like that. However, if the government does decide that they will make playing numbers legal, then we should leave the casinos for the tourist let them enjoy themselves, because some Bahamian will only go in the casinos and cause problems for themselves and act like fools. In my opinion it is a no, no, for Bahamians to be allowed into hotel casinos.

We as a people need to move forward and start accepting change, because the only way the government can make it better for us is to have revenue flowing into the treasury at all times from inside the country and out of the country. If or when they do legalize numbers and the lottery they should remember that it should be owned one hundred percent by Bahamians.

This is another way that we can make our economy strong and keep putting money into the treasury and into the hands of poor people because the fact of the matter is that the poor do most of the spending and spending is what keeps the economy going strong. I think if the government makes playing numbers legal the treasury will see about $50 million dollars a year if it is done right. Listen people let's start doing things the right way for a change.

And for the record I can't find anywhere in the Bible where it says that playing numbers is wrong, unlike drinking rum and getting drunk which the Bible does say is wrong. Unfortunately drinking rum is legal and many people lose their lives each year from drinking rum so what does that say to the people of the country.

REGULATION FOR AUTO DEALERS

If you drive around Nassau, you would see all the old broken down cars in people's yards, some of the cars have garbage in them and it's like people don't care to move their cars even though the government sprays a warning on the cars saying that they should move the cars before a particular time. This makes the yards look like a dump; these people have no pride in themselves and their surroundings. At least someone is taking the old cars and making money off of them through the scrap metal trade. There are about one or two places in Nassau that take the old cars and crush them down and ship them out of the country, this helps to relieve the overflow of old cars that take up space and make the country look downright nasty.

We need a new law to be made to deal with the cars, trucks and motor bikes, like the ruthless people who bring in the junk title cars, trucks and jeeps. These are the same vehicles that are not allowed on the road in the U.S. but they bring the cars here and fix them back to about 85% of their original state. The U.S. calls these vehicles salvage vehicles and unrebuildable title cars and they can only be shipped out of the country or used for parts. The U.S. does this with motor bikes also. So here is what I think we should do about this.

No used cars, trucks, vans or jeeps should be allowed into the country with an unrebuildable title, the government should not allow any used cars in the country that are older than four years old, not from the U.S. or Japan. If the used vehicles are

less than four years old the cars must have a rebuild title or what they also call a clean title and all the important parts on the vehicles must be replaced, such as airbags, the seatbelts and all the that is necessary to rebuild the vehicles and keep the owners safe. Any parts that were damaged in the accident they must be replaced with new parts so the cars can pass inspection. Airbags and seatbelts should be standard, no new car dealer should be able to sell used vehicles unless the car was a trade in vehicle, we must make this a level playing field for new and used cars dealers alike.

No off name brand vehicles should be allowed into the country as there are no licensed auto dealers who can provide parts for them. The new cars dealers should only be allowed to sell two different types of name brand cars to allow room for growth in the country.

Do you realize that there are about forty to fifty new and used cars dealers in Nassau alone and each car lot has about fifty to one hundred cars on their lot? That means Nassau is becoming overwhelmed with all these car lots and there are no rules for these dealers, the government needs to take a proactive approach to this before it becomes a big problem for us.

By putting in rules and guidelines for new and used car dealers it will make it better for them because the government is leveling the playing field for all of them, new and used car dealers alike whether they admit to it or not. It's not about one dealer it's about them all, that they stay in business and keep people employed so the economy can continue growing and be stronger and keep the money circulating in the country.

Another thing the government can do is look at cutting the duty on new cars, trucks and vans from the dealers so hard working people who pay their taxes can afford to buy a nice new vehicle, it's not like the government is losing all the duties on new vehicles if they were to cut down the duty.

They would only be losing just a little of the duty money and by cutting the duties and making a deal with new car dealers, this will insure that people will spend their money at home in the Bahamas. Here is an example of what I'm talking about, let us say a new Toyota Camry cost $18,000 from the manufacturer and the government duty is 85% of that, so the total is $33,600 with shipping and then the dealer must put on their mark up to make a profit so the price of the Camry is $43,995. However if the duties were dropped to 60%, the price of that Camry would be $30,400. With shipping plus 27% mark up, that there is good for the people so that they can shop at home and that's the whole idea, to get Bahamians to shop at home. Sure you might say that the government is losing revenue by cutting 25% off of the customs duty, and I agree that it is a lot, but the government will make it back in other places like if the government were to put income and company taxes into the law and enforce it. If we do this the country can progress and the people can move forward and keep up with the rest of the world because we are at least 30 steps behind a lot of counties and that does not speak well for us.

Let us move forward Bahamas and implement income and company taxes so that the government will be able to do these things with no problem. Remember now it's about giving and taking, the government takes a little and gives a lot, a little is income and company taxes and by giving the people breaks on custom duties and other things it will keep the economy strong. The only way that any of this can work is by all of us working together for a better Bahamas.

LABOUR BOARD & MINIMUM WAGE

You know what eats me alive, when the rich or the people who own their business take advantage of their good, hard working employees and treat them like nothing, and when you go and report them to the labor board that's when the long fight begins. This battle could be long and insufferable, just so you can get what is owed to you by law, and that's if you ever get it. Sometimes some of the people don't deserve it at all. If you ask labor officers what is their goal when they have a labor matter before them and listen to what they say carefully, it will sound good but is that what they really try to achieve?

The labor board needs to be reformed, reorganized and rebuilt. For starters, three or four of the labor officers need to be removed, and one or two need to retired, they should know who they are. Many of the officers need to have more training so that they can deal with cases that come before them more decisively and the government should give the labor board more power to settle cases more efficiently.

I personally have my experiences with the labor board, and let the truth be known, I must say again that some of the officers need to be removed from that department. I do not want to say anything bad about the labor department and I'll try not to, but if the officers and the ministry say that there is nothing wrong within the labor department, then you know that there is something really wrong without a doubt. Either that or they might say that there are one or two things that need to be charged or fixed. We the people of the Bahamas need and depend on the labor board to get satisfaction for us, monies that belong to us by law from what I call "life sucking vampires" who use and abuse the poor people of the Bahamas just because they have money. Yes I said it, life sucking vampires. That does not mean all employers but for whom the cap fits let them wear it; I call it like I see it. My opinion is biased against some of the officers at the labor board so I can't get into more details as I would like to and it would be unfair to the good officers and the whole department. I did say that I will not say anything bad about the labor department because of the good work that they are mandated to do for the people of the Bahamas. And I know you might be thinking that I should tell you my experience so that I could shed light on some of the problems but that is for another time and place. The problems will manifest themselves when the leader goes and looks for them.

I only have one more thing to say on this topic and that is that the labor department needs to be reformed, empowered, and to be cemented in the fight for poor people's rights. Can someone give them a pay increase please? Amen

MINIMUM WAGE

The simple fact of the matter is that minimum wage needs to be increased to about $250.00 dollar a week, because food has gone up, and gas has gone up, so high it was almost $7.00 dollar a gallon in the past. It is now back down but who knows went it will go back up even higher. When we take into account single parents, mothers and fathers and the fact that daycare went up, the light bills and cooking gas has gone up, all these things play a big role in day to day living for poor people. By increasing the minimum wage to $250.00 dollars a week or what would be forty hours a week that means that poor people can eat little better and live a little better. Remember, there is enough money to go around, so if companies' say that they cannot afford this $250.00 dollar for minimum wage they should close their doors because we can't keep having this same mentality of getting something for nothing. A lot of big companies like it that way give a little and get a whole lot from their staff. The only way those companies would be able to work around this is by cutting the hours to match the pay, but that means that their work will take longer to get done so think about it, if the government can pay the people who clean the streets $250.dollars a week, I am sure the private companies can. In fact some companies are doing it already and I hope the government looks into this long and hard.

THE POLICE FORCE

Can someone tell me, what is the mandate of the police force in the Bahamas? I know what it should be for a police force in a democratic country, but what is the mandate for this country? I think the best persons to ask that question to would be a young police officer because some of the older officers who have more years on the force might have forgotten, not all of them but many of them. The young offices should know what their mandate is because they have just finished the police college and basic training. Can you do me a big favor when you see a police officer ask him, what is your mandate as a police officer? It should be to protect and service the public and uphold the laws of the Bahamas at all cost, that is a part of every country that has a democratic government.

Now, the question is do all of the police officers on the force uphold these laws? Let me tell you what I've seen officers do in my time. Remember now I am not calling any names so I am not carrying any blame. In my personal experiences, I have seen police officers take money from questionable people, I have seen officers drinking on the job, I have seen officers using bad language on the job and in public, I have seen officers with illegal guns and drugs, I have seen officers shoot unarmed persons and get away with it, I have seen an officer get away with having sex with underage girls. What should I say about that? Here is another incident that I know of. A sergeant was charged with having sex with his fourteen and fifteen year old daughters and one of them ended up being pregnant for him. In October and November of 2009 there were

two diffident police offices in the news charge with having sex with an underage children. Can you believe that? My reaction was "what in the hell is going on around here"? I only have one question to ask, where are the parent or parents of these kids? I have also heard from officers that they have seen other officers plant fake evidence. And then there are officers who have been brought up on charges of rape, murder, stealing, taking bribes, selling and trafficking drugs, and I can go on and on. I think you get the picture as clear as day, and I believe for many of you I am telling you things you already know but I don't want you to forget what is going on in this country. What is sad is that some of these offices would get charged with one of these crimes or offences and ninety percent of the time you will never hear anything about it again. Now that is corruption!

That is what they do. They who, you might ask? The police and the government just sweep things under the carpet, behind closed doors they'll say don't worry about it we'll just sweep it under the rug and the people will forget about it. To them it is a simple thing and the easiest thing to do. Remember what I said in the beginning of this book about corruption, it goes in and out up and down round and round and throughout the system. You know the old saying that one bad apple spoils the whole bunch, so imagine what a hand full of bad apples would do on the police force.

I remember one time ago I heard senior police officers who had just retried say this about the force, that 20% of the police force is corrupted and 20% are normal and can go either way and the other 60% are good and not corrupt. That is from a retired police officers mouth. Who knows what goes on in the house better then the people who live there, I know some people and police officers alike will be foaming at the mouth when they read this but if you are not a part of this corrupt 20% then you should not be mad about it. Remember what i said many times, "who the caps fit let them where it". Thankfully the force is going through some positive changes and a lot of the top officers are being given their retirement packages and laws are being put into place to change the way the police forces does things. The sad part about that is a small change will not make much of a difference because the police force needs to be over hauled because that is the only way the force will make a big difference in the communities. It seems as if no one has respect for the police anymore and that is a shame that the people who they are mandated to protect and serve do not have any respect for the police.

I can remember when we were children and you would hear that a police officer was coming and you would run home and hide from them as if you did something wrong. The police at that time received all the respect in the world from adults, teenagers and children alike.

The police force's presence was felt in all of the over the hill communities and some days the older people could not wait for the police to come through their corner so that they can talk to them and give them food or something to drink to show that they care and to thank them for just being around the community. I am afraid that those days are long gone, and that is sad!

So what do we do about this? Here are some of the things that I think need to be discontinued. If any officers say to you that these things don't happen then you know what that officer is talking right, pure foolishness. One of these things that need to stop is the beating of persons in police custody. We must stop covering up and protecting officers that are breaking the law. Officers need to stop taking money from people, using bad language in public, and must show respect for the public who they protect and serve. As I think about it I could go on and on all day about these things but as I see it the only way to cut down on the slackness, foolishness and corruption is to reorganize the police force and make some new rules with hard penalties for them. Not because they are police officers does that mean they are all good and honest officers, whoever tells you that you should tell them that is a lie from the pit of hell and if you believe that you need to get your head examined. They are going through a transition at the top of the police force but that is not good enough, we the people of the Bahamas need the police force to be overhauled, take out and get rid of the bad apples or at least 95% of them that give the police force a bad name.

I personally think that only one man and his team can send ripples through the police force and weed out the bad apples. That is the main thing that needs to change, because too much foolishness is going on in the police force. The bad apples think that they are untouchable and they can do and say whatever they want under the cover of darkness. After saying all of that, please, do not get me wrong, I'm not trying to bring down the police force because really and truly these are the people who protect and serve us.

Many officers do an excellent job for the people and the Bahamas and I would personally like to thank the hard working officers who put their lives on the line twenty four seven, three hundred sixty five days a year for me and everyone else in the Bahamas. Let me prove my case and point, in the news report and news paper dated 11th of February 2009 it stated that there were reports of police officers from the drug unit selling drugs and cocaine on the streets and being paid to lose or destroy evidence and criminal files. Most of us know or assume that the report can't be far from the truth. The report also indicated that they want the public to report such officers to the Commissioner of police. This is noble but let's be reasonable, there is no way in this world that the police can police, the police. I would dare say not one hundred percent effectively and perhaps not even fifty percent, there is no way.

That would be like one brother who is a police officer coming to lockup his two brothers and one sister in front of his mother and father, aunts and uncles and cousins. I am sure you would agree

that, that will never work because the police force is like one big family. I wish anyone good luck trying to get family to talk on family so I say good luck getting the police to police themselves. Sometimes it seems to me like every police officer is doing his or her own thing on the police force and they do not answer to the superior officers in charge. Or is it that they don't care and don't want to listen to the inspectors, superintendents and ACP's and maybe even the Commissioner of police. My view on it is we all have to answer to someone and someone has to lead, and If you don't love and respect your job as a police man or woman then you should have not become one and you should get out. It seems like a lot of police officers have a chip on their shoulder and we don't need officers like that on the force. We need officers who will protect and serve and uphold the law and show respect for the general public, not people who just want a government job so that they can be secure as far as having a job that is not good enough.

In concluding this topic, think of what you would like to see the police force become and how do you see the police force now. Remember this, these officers are paid to protect and serve us and to uphold the law, they are not I say not doing us any favors they are doing their jobs that they applied for, and we the people are paying them to do that job. I would like to see the police force one day get back the respect that they lost and become a good and upstanding organization that it was and is meant to be because if the police force does not have any respect for the general public and the uniform that they wear and the laws that they promise to uphold, then we are lost as a country.

NEW INTELLIGENCE AGENCY

Do you know the old saying, when the cat is away the mouse will come and play? Well there is no cat and the mouse are running rampant in the house, taking what they want, and doing what they want when they want and wreaking havoc in the house. Let me explain this analogy to you, the mouse are the police and the house is the country and the cat is the new intelligence agency, who would keep the police in order and in check, but since there is no cat the mouse are doing what they want. I am not saying that the police are rats; this was just an analogy.

The bad apples in the police force are running rampant in this country, and I know the people in charge of the force would say that it's not as bad as I am or other people are making it out to be. This may be okay but the truth is, the more you deny and hide it the worst the problem will become, remember that I said it. Let me say this again not all of the police force is corrupt, I would guess that about 20 to 30 percent of the force is corrupt although it could be more or it could be less. Whatever the number is, remember that analogy of the one bad apple spoils the whole bunch and that is only one apple so think about what 20 to 30 percent can do to the force. The fact of the matter is there is a dark cloud over the police force and its building up for a thunder storm.

Most of the big countries have a cat to keep the mouse in check. In the United States for example the internal affairs unit of the FBI, England has one, France has one, and Scotland has one and so on. Most of these big countries have another level of police or an intelligence agency to police the police and to police the government officials who are caught up in corruption. We are not as big as those other countries but we need this agency just as much as they need theirs because the corruption is just as big as theirs or bigger. So where is the Bahamas intelligence agency that is responsible for keeping the outlaws and people who think that they are above the law from taking over this country?

This agency will protect the people from the corrupt police, immigration officers, government officials and the most hardened and dangerous criminals. I know you might say that this is too farfetched, but I don't think so, and we the people of this country need this agency because if we don't implement this soon, then this country will fall by the way side with corruption. Remember the police are a mob whether a good mob or a bad mob, they have authority in the country and if 75% of the police force decides to go bad we are in big problems. That of course is just the worst case scenario. Now I know you would like to know how we are going to pay for this agency, the answer is in the first chapter in this book.

How do we get this agency started? First we start small by hand picking qualified high school students in grade 12 that are smart, driven and ready to take on their destiny, then we send them off for training with the FBI and Interpol and I'm sure if we ask our friends in these agencies for their help they would be more than happy to help us with training for our men and women. We should let the men and women train for about five years and then bring them back home and slowly put this agency together and I am sure within ten years this agency can be up and running. With the help of Interpol and the U.S government we will create a strong intelligence agency against crime and corruption and this agency can be used for dealing with anything that is illegal when it comes to government. This agency should have its own Judges assigned to deal with cases so that there will be no waiting three and four years to have a case come up. This agency will only answer to the P.M. and the Minister of Defense no one else, and this agencies mandate will be to clean up the evilness and corruption in this country.

The other day I was watching footage from a wake on T.V for the young man who was killed by the police in the area between Village and Kemp road and I think the young man's name was Brenton Hector Smith. I do not know whether the shooting was a clean shooting or not, that remains to be seen at this time and at the end of the court case it will be revealed, but at this wake the minister of defense Mr. Tommy Turnquest was giving his speech and in his speech he said that the laws of the Bahamas are there to police the police also. My thought was wait, wait, wait a minute, did he just say what I think he just said in the front of all of those people, let me quote it again, the laws of the

Bahamas are there to police the police, when he said that I thought that I was hearing things but that's what he said and if the laws of the Bahamas are there to police the police then who is going to enforce it because the police are there to enforce the laws when it comes to the general public so who is enforcing the law for the police. I really want you to think about it and tell me what I'm missing? This is where the new agency comes into play. There is only a small group of people that I can see who would disagree with this and say that we do not need a new agency like this and those people would include corrupt police officers, some M.P's and people who have no idea about what is going on in the Bahamas and around them, don't care at all and who live in their own world. Not only will this be good for the progress of the Bahamas, but this agency will be the ace in the hole for the people of the Bahamas. In addition to this, I would say to those people who would say no, they do not agree with having an agency like this, remember those words from President BARACK OBAMA, and Nas the rapper it goes like this, "yes we can, be what we want to be, if we work hard at it, there will be no stopping us".

CUBA

Cuba, the sleeping giant of the Caribbean, this country is vast as we all know, and the Bahamas can sit in Cuba many times over. Cuba is interesting but before I continue let me tell you this about my experience in Cuba. Man on the way to Cuba we were approaching and were about to land on the runway in Havana and it was amazing seeing that beautiful landscape and the lush green fields, it made me feel so at home in Cuba. I almost wanted to hop out of the plane and jump over the fence and take off all my clothes and run through the green fields feeling free as the day I was born, climb some coconut trees and live in the bush for a couple of days. That's the way I was feeling when I came into Cuba, it reminded me so much of what home used to be like, the serenity of the place. By the way I didn't go to Cuba for the women, I went to discover Cuba and to see all that Cuba had to offer like the Cuban culture and the food. I cannot forget the food, my mouth is watering just thinking about the food, and the sexy mojitos drinks. The women are beautiful also but this is not about them, even though they are a part of the culture.

I realized that Cuba has so much to offer because of its size and its hard working people, hundreds of miles of beach front and millions of acres of untouched land and lot of small islands around Cuba. The people are really nice to one another and put family first and hard work next, I remember when we used to be like that where we put God first then family and then hard work. Those good old days in the Bahamas, I miss them so much, the love and camaraderie was a blessing, we use to live like that but we lost it somewhere in the generations. You might say Cuba does not have anything on us, if this is the way you are thinking you need to tell me what country you are living in because you cannot be referring to the Bahamas. Let me take you down memory lane just for a minute. Over sixty years ago when the Bahamas was a good place and safe place to be in and live in, Cuba was exploding with investors from all over the world and Havana was the place to be in the Caribbean, it was also like a small country by itself, remember now this was when Cuba was open to the U.S and all of the fast money making people were in Cuba or going to setup in Cuba. Havana was the rich man's delight and a joy for middle class and it was only one and a half hours away by airplane. It was so easy to go to Cuba for the weekend to party and gamble the weekend away. In those times I heard Cuba was an exciting and wonderful place to be and even though Cuba has changed a whole lot, remember this, the more things change the more they stay the same. What I mean by this is that through all their problems with the U.S. including being black listed by the US and other countries, their economy falling into ruins, almost going to war with U.S and yet despite all of that trouble, Cuba also has income tax.

Many other things remain the same like their culture for example. The Cuban culture remains deeply rooted in family, hard work food and dance. One day Cuba is going to become very important to the Caribbean.

PROGRESS

What I mean when I say that is they will be able to supply all of Caribbean's needs as far as food is concerned. I can see it now they have the man power, the land and their ability to do it. Let us say example that Cuba was to start a large farming industry and they just farm live stock like pigs, cows, chickens, goats, sheep and fish along with products like eggs and milk for export at a good price to the surrounding Caribbean counties. Where would we be in this picture? We would be buying from other people again when we can do all of these things for ourselves. Do not forget that Cuba is in the Caribbean also, just take a look at Cuba on the map and its size, to open a farming industry like this would be very easy for Cuba to do. You might ask where they will get the money from. The same place a lot of other countries get their money from, China, the World Bank and investors. If other countries can get hundreds of billions from China and China only gets back interest on that money, imagine the Chinese getting interest on their money and access to new lands in a country right next to the U.S. For some of their Chinese people you cannot beat that with a stick, that would be a very desirable deal for the Chinese and they would lend the money to the Cubans because that is good business.

I am sure you have seen that China and the Bahamas have become good friends over the years and the Chinese have given the Bahamas a lot of money. You might also be aware that the Chinese are building us a new 30 million dollar stadium for what they say is free.

If the Chinese are befriending us like this can you imagine how they will act towards Cuba.

You might ask what about the embargo on Cuba? I would not advise you to worry about that, because it will not be long until the embargo will be lifted, you can mark my words on that. Like some of us Bahamians say "it een long now", the fresh wind will be blowing soon for Cuba. I do not know if you remember when the U.S president came in to power what he did? He lifted some of the restrictions on travelling to Cuba from the U.S. Trust me on this one when I say Cuba will be fully opened to the U.S.A if not in this term then the next term. Let us face it; it's going to happen believe it or not. As a case and point we all knew one day that there was going to be a black president of the United State. Dr. Martin Luther king Jr. at that time had that wonderful dream, may God bless is soul and may Dr. King rest in peace, but we did not think that it was going to happen in our life time or in this generation. That is evidence of the power of my God, one minute there is no strong black leader and the next minute a strong black God fearing man became president of the United States of America. This happened right out of the blue and you can see how it caught us all off guard so imagine when Cuba opens up? Hopefully you see my point.

My goal is to open up your eyes to the things that you cannot see. Notice how quickly Barack Obama became president, almost overnight and when Cuba opens up it will feel like it happened overnight. The only thing left for the leader to do is to sit down and talk and to lift the ban off Cuba, and you might say "that" will never happen not in my or your life time. If that is your thought read the part about Barack Obama in this paragraph again.

Let us get back to the issue of Cuba being the provider to the surrounding Caribbean countries and that day might come when Cuba becomes one of the biggest exporters of fruits and vegetables and meats to all the countries around "her". When this happens the U.S and a lot of other countries will come and buy from Cuba especially if they start making quality products at a good price. The Bahamas will sink like the titanic and we will not be able to sell that dream of sun sand and sea to the other people in the world anymore because they will say why go to the Bahamas and Cuba is right there and Cuba has sun sand and sea also, cheaper prices more places to go and Cuba has a lot of beautiful women and a richer culture and that is just the tip of the ice berg. So why go to the Bahamas again? Just for the so called friendly Bahamian people, I don't think so. I am not putting down the Bahamians because I am one and the Bahamas is my home also. I am two hundred percent Bahamian and I love my country two hundred percent and I love my people half of the time because you know how we Bahamians go. I love being in the Bahamas too. My point is that I have to let you know what we are up against and why we have to take our head out of the sand so we can truly see what's going on around us. I am not boasting about Cuba, I am just pointing out some of things that Cuba has to offer and their capabilities.

Cuba and the Bahamas are like a race between a man in a car and a man on a bicycle. The Bahamas is the person on the bicycle and Cuba is the person driving the car and the car hasn't even started yet but the person on the bicycle is just riding round and round in circles, so when the person in the car gets started who do you think will cross the finish line first to win? The funny thing is Cuba or the man in the car gave the man on the bicycle a fifty year head start? I will tell you this, it does not look like you should put your money on the man on the bicycle. Bahamians have so much to offer, and the potential to do so much good for this country and its people but it remains to be seen what will be done by the leaders of this country. That is one of the reasons why I wrote this book so that you can read about it, so you can see it with your own eyes, so you can hear it with your own ears. If after all of this and you don't do any of these things that are in this book, that is okay because this book will always be there to say I told you so.

ANDROS

O my Andros she big she big she big she big so they say she big. Andros, a vast and beautiful body of land that is a big part of the Bahamas and its people, from the regattas and the home coming and going out fishing and crabbing in the night, it's a down home thing and it's a whole lot of fun, from having one or two cold ones to some good crab n rice or crab n grits, that's the first thing I go looking for when I hit the airport in Andros. Some crab n' rice with snapper and plantain, man my mouth done start watering. Let us put that aside and focus on the things Andros has to offer or what I see Andros has to officer. Let me say this first of all, we do not need to worry about Cuba opening up at all, once we start putting these things that are needed into place to prepare and insure a strong and dependable economy for the future of the Bahamas and its people. This may sound like a contradiction but it is not.

Andros could become a great place to live, don't get me wrong it is ok now, but Andros is big enough for a nice sized city like Nassau and an industrial park where industrial buildings and warehouses are. It is big enough for a farming industry, it is big enough for highway like I-95, it is big enough for residential communities and gated communities, and even a fast train running from north Andros to South Andros along with big shopping malls and hotels but we must plan it all out on paper first. Let me tell you about my vision for Andros, have you ever been to a big city where the air is clean and it looks clean all around you, and the city feels good to be in because of its surroundings. This is what I see in my vision for Andros, a good size city in the heart of Andros where it is clean and beautiful with tall colonial buildings and monuments to honor our fore fathers and the father of nation. Somewhere where there are clean and green parks where people take their kids and their pets where basket ball courts and baseball fields are, where young people can go have fun, a city full of serenity and with far less crime. Have you ever been to Toronto, Vancouver British Columbia or Montreal Canada, if not, you definitely need to go so you can see what I mean. If you have been you will know what I am talking about. I wish I could email or text my vision to your brain from my brain so you can see the Andros I am picturing in my head. I know you might say that I have too many big dreams and no money!!! That may be true I don't have the money but it is right here in this county you just need to know where to look and how to get it. Throughout this book I will show you from start to finish where to find money in this country, because there is no shortage of money in this country or this world.

Besides that, if you don't set goals you cannot achieve them. Dr. King had a dream and it came to pass. President Barack Obama had a dream and it came true and I'm sure you had a dream also that might have come true. A lot of my hopes and dreams came through by the love, grace and goodness of my Heavenly Farther, all thanks unto God for his love for us. So to say to me my dream or vision for Andros is too farfetched or imposable it would be a clear contradiction of what black people have achieved. As another case and point, let us look at the country of Dubai. One minute it is just a desert and the next minute a city out of the sand. One day Andros is going to be a big and beautiful and wonderful city, with people from all walks of life and she will give back to us what we put in, I just hope I live to see it and be a part of it. I want to be able to walk down the street to Bamboo shack, wait a minute they better have Bamboo shack there I mean right in the heart of the city. You know I will be right there at the window ordering my conch snack, one conch snack please with extra hot sauce and ketchup, this is what I hope for, my vision and my dream for Andros. You can only use this vision if you are going to do something with it and let's make the Bahamas one of the best places in the world to live.

MY OBSERVATION

This morning I woke up on the wrong side of the floor. Not really but that's just how I felt. I had to ask myself why I am writing this book again. The reason why I asked myself this question is because if you stop and listen to the news and what is going on in the country and if you were me you would probably say I am not wasting my time with this book because no one is going to listen. For an example, on November 15th 2009 I had stopped to get me some good Bahamian food and I missed and told the lady to put the TV on channel 11 news and as soon as she had put the TV on channel 11 the bad news came at me like I had my phone turned off and I had just turned it back on. It was like I had missed twenty text messages. I said that to say this is how fast the bad news came at me, it was crazy, one policeman got shot and a defense force officer was killed for trying to stop two men from fighting and at least five gun crimes were committed in the space of three days. Two weeks later what would be the first week in December two police officers were charged with raping a woman, and at the end of 2009 the country logged 86 murders.

This is one of the reasons why I like China and Cuba because there is far, far, less crime and murders. Most people are just going about their day to day business. When I was is in China I saw one fight, it was four men attacking one man and then the police pulled up and the two police got out of the jeep and locked up all five of the men and here is the funny part, the police put all five of them in the jeep with only one police officer and he pulled off with them and they had no handcuffs on and there was no fighting or rowing in the jeep. Me and the other Bahamians were amazed by this. Something like that would not be happen here anytime soon.

I would really hate it if I have to move to another country because the crime is out of control and getting worse, because I live my life enjoying the peaceful and beautiful day God has given us. I love to live for today and let tomorrow take care of itself and in the meantime prepare for the future but how can a person live their life in peace when it seems like the people who are committing these crimes are stuck on stupid and foolishness. While you as a person are trying to live the right way people like these are trying to walk all over you. That is one of the reasons someone has to document what is going on in this country in a book, and give the people some sense of hope for the future. I guess so far that person would be me?

As you can see even I get discouraged too sometimes but I will not let the evil that I see and hear prevent me from finishing this book, because this is my gift that my God has given me to do. Starting this book is like breaking down a water dam, once the water starts running it is almost impossible to stop. I know one thing, I'm ready to get back on the plane and take me some crab n' rice, crack conch and boil and fry fish with me and live in love and serenity with no worrying about if someone is going to kill me for something I said or something that belongs to me. Life is becoming too, too, hard in the Bahamas and I am only trying to live and enjoy my life and live out my liberty my God has given me.

NEW & CLEAN FORMS OF ENERGY

Once again it seems like we as Bahamians are behind the 8 ball when it comes to doing anything good for the country and its people because we are far behind with going green for a small country. We should have been on the front line when it comes to clean and green energy, the reason why I said that is because we are up with technology in every aspect of our life like energy star TV's, refrigerators, washers and dryers, energy saving light bulbs, air-conditioners, telecommunications, fax machines, computers the internet and it does not stop.

When it comes to going green with supplying the energy to the country we are far behind. Going green with clean cars and clean energy and ways to make energy and to import the stuff we need is very easy for the Bahamas because of our size.

See the world started out green with Adam & Eve from then right up to the 1800's when all of that changed with the industrial revolution. We are going right back there; me and millions of people know that this is the way to go. Let me prove it to you. If you could have a party without your house being destroyed, would you have it? Or if you could drive a car without damaging the ozone, would you? If we can have clean energy without the deadly toxins that cause cancer and other health problems don't you think we should have that in the country? I think so and that's my opinion. Clean energy was designed by God and given to man to develop for our use. I hope you don't think man came up with this energy thing by themselves, (see proverbs 8:12 and you will see what I mean). For a small country, the Bahamas has tons of money coming in and out of it every day and we cannot seem to get started with going green.

To me that makes no sense and what makes it worse is that the Prime Minster of the country said we are going green or the goal is to become green. He said this himself in front of the world. To me that is the same thing. Some might say that it is easier said than done but I disagree. I will show you how it is done. First you put in the budget every year two million dollars for two wind turbines with no duty added because this is for the betterment of the country. We buy them and install them in key places like Harbor Island because they really need a stable energy supply over there. It does not matter where you put them they will spin and make power and piece by piece we will slowly put the turbines on all the islands and in the right places that need them the most. In ten years we would have 20 of the wind turbines in key places so we can stop depending so much on fuel run generators that break down from working so hard. Do you know that Jamaica has wind turbines already; I saw them with my own eyes about fifty of them in Manchester on a hill overlooking the ocean. What does that say about us?

A wind turbine is like a giant alternator, once the turbine continues to spin it makes clean energy, you can't beat that with a stick. The wind turbines are one of the best ways to go for the islands and maybe the city also, that's my opinion. The wind does not stop blowing out there on the ocean front, the wind turbine seems to me to be the cleanest and the safest type of energy next to solar panel energy and I know that there are other ways to get clean energy but I'm only talking about this one because it is perfect for the size of our country. Whatever the government plans on doing about clean energy, I really hope they seek a lot of wise counsel about which type of clean energy is best for the Bahamas. Remember it is better to be clean and green than to live in a nasty dump of a country.

RECYCLING

It looks to me like some Bahamians are doing what they can to recycle and they are making a living and good business out of recycling, which is excellent, they recycle metals, tires and beer bottles. From what I can see so far they are making a good living out of recycling and I love to see my people doing the right thing even if it's for money, every bit helps.

As for the government doing what they can to recycle, it looks like another snail crossing the road, the snail thinks it is moving very fast but we know that it is not. If I was in charge I would build a large building on two or three acres of crown land just for recycling paper, metals, cans, plastics bottles, glass, styrofoam, cardboard boxes, and old electronics. There are lots more things that can be recycled that people throw away and it goes right to the dump and become bio hazardous materials and it damages the ground and the drinking water supply. The good part about this is we don't even have to literally recycle these things here in the Bahamas; all we need to do is separate the garbage from the recyclable product and package them so that they can be shipped off to a big recycling plant in the US so they can be recycled properly.

Now I don't know if the recycling plant pays for plastic, styrofoam, cardboard boxes, paper, and old electronics, but I do know that we can't keep going the way we are going now just putting it all in the dump. These things or products take a very long time to break down and dissolve and some of them don't break down at all, and I'm sure you know this by now; the garbage has to go somewhere. I believe we should put the garbage in the dump and recyclable product will be sent to the recycling building to be separated and shipped off. This building that I was talking about that I think the government should build will in my opinion provide jobs for lots of people so that they can provide for themselves. It is a dirty job but someone has to do it. And by the way did you see how high the dump is getting, drive by sometime on Gladstone road and take a look at it.

If the big recycling plants do pay for the stuff we send to them that would be excellent because that is money that can help pay some of the overhead if not all of it. Whether the big recycling plants pay for these things or not, that is not the issue the goal is to recycle and keep the Bahamas clean while at the same time putting people to work. We have to start somewhere!! Now I know you want to ask where the money would be coming from. Good thinking. If you read the first chapter of this book or if you read the chapter on the numbers racket in the Bahamas, you would see where the money could come from to build this recycling building.

Let us point out a fact, one of ten richest self-made women on the planet made her money by recycling paper. She is listed in Forbes magazine list of the richest women in the world or if you just Google her name, Ms. Yan Cheung is worth an estimated $1.7 billion dollars.

Do you realize that most of the answers and solutions that I have been giving in this book have in it a part on hiring people and keeping the economy strong? When people are working and they pay their bills and buy food and spend money on other things that's what makes an economy strong, when people buy and sell stuff. Keeping the Bahamas clean is in all of our best interest; it's not too late to start and if you are already recycling keep it up and may God bless you for all your good works.

THE CHURCH

Remember back in the days when the church bus used to come and pick you up from home after school, and you would go and do something good in church or have bible study or choir practice and on Wednesday it would be game night and on Thursday it would be youth meeting and it would run right into Sunday?

This was week in and week out, I personally did love it and so did my older sisters. Can someone please tell me what happened to that, that commitment to the church? Church members and their children being active and I am not just talking about one church I am talking about most of them. It seems today like they have stopped doing all of these different things in the church.

It also seems like only the Haitian churches and one or two others are still doing these things every week. With the other churches it remains to be seen because I do not see very much going on in recent times. Perhaps if they stop getting in the governments business and stay focused on God's word and teaching it to the people like they are supposed to then more can be accomplished. I believe that knowledge is power and by teaching the people, they would know more about God and be able to make better choices and decisions when it comes to their faith in God and in their lives. Too many churches today seem to want to be mixed up in things that don't concern them, what should concern them is God's word and his people and taking care of God's people until our Lord and Savior returns.

This is the mandate for the church that they should go out into the world and teach and preach the word of God to the ends of the earth. This is the mandate that was left for the leaders, namely the Bishops, Pastors, Priests and anybody who has a big title and stands in front of the church to teach or preach. I would like to see one of these persons stand up and say that this is not one of the mandates for the church. You see this thing is like an assembly line, if the church stops what they are doing to focus on what the government is doing then who is going to do what the church is supposed to be doing? Please don't get me wrong the government should ask the church for its opinion about important matters from time to time. By this I mean their opinion, not telling the government what to do because the government should always seek wise counsel whether it is from the people or the church or persons who have knowledge about the issues at hand. The church and government do not exist for their own best interest, but the church is for the people's best interest in Christ Jesus and government is there for the people's best interest when it comes to the country, am I right or wrong?

Jesus tells us about the false prophets and that they will have their reward for leading the people astray. The church has been around from Jesus left earth and he left instruction on what the church should be doing, so don't you think the church should be one of the most organized pillars of society, yes or no? Why am I going so deep with this? The reason is that in the church there is so much foolishness and foulness going on. For example some of the women in church are sleeping with the leaders of the church, the leaders of the church are having homosexual activity, the leaders of the church are having sex with young boys and young girls and sometimes money goes missing from the church's bank account. In some of these cases where the money went missing only them and God knows. In some cases I am talking about hundreds of thousands of dollars just disappearing. In today's world this almost looks like a good business to be in. Sometimes the thought comes to mind that I might as well open a church but

I have to quickly catch myself because I am not going to lead God's people astray just for money and power because there is only one true power and that is God. Now if any of this does not apply to you or your church then the cap does not fit you and you don't have anything to worry about. Every man and woman has to be responsible for their own soul and the dirt that they are doing.

I am very disappointed in the church. You might say who am I to tell the church that I am disappointed in them!! I am a child of God who is the head of the church, they have clearly forgotten this because of the things they do and actions speak louder than words. Proverbs 24:16 says that a just man may fall seven times, and rise up again, but the wicked shall fall into mischief. Also see proverbs 15:3. I looked in the bible for this chapter and read it for yourself. I implore you to read the whole book of proverbs and I believe your mind will be opened and your heart will be pleased. Some of the church leaders have fallen deep in mischief and they cannot tell day from night but it doesn't matter what they do, I must let them know that my God cannot be mocked, the bible says this. In spite of this I do not want to keep talking about what they are doing wrong instead let us talk about what we can do to fix the problems that the leaders of the churches are faced with. My goal is always about fixing the problems rather than to keep talking about them. I was not judging them either, just pointing out what is going on with some of the churches and the people in the church. If you deny that these things happen in some of the churches you are lying to yourself.

Once again we see the church putting its nose where it doesn't belong in the government's business. On May 26th 2010 the Prime Minster was about to make the number racket legal in the country but church leaders decided they must have something to say about this!!! They stated that this is a Christian nation and playing numbers or gambling is wrong because people will take their whole paycheck and spend it in the number houses and society will become morally bankrupt.

That is what they say will happen if gambling is made legal, that is it in a nut shell. My question is who are they to tell a person how and where to spend their paycheck? They did not work for it and my paycheck does not belong to them so how can they tell me how to spend it. Think about this aspect of it, playing numbers was illegal and still is illegal but people are still playing numbers and the government isn't getting any tax money from the number houses so legal or illegal, playing numbers isn't going to stop any time soon and the forty to fifty million dollars the government was going to get has been stopped by the church and others.

I am wondering if the church leaders can pay that forty or fifty million dollars a year to the government in taxes so that the government does not have to even look at that tax money from the number houses. Perhaps they can pay it; perhaps that is just a walk in the park for them.

Whatever government decides to do in the country the church should not have a direct say in matters that don't concern them. If gambling did concern them they would have made a final decision on it a long time ago. This is not their decision to make it is the government and the people's decision to make. Unless an until this is placed in front of you to deal with, it doesn't concern you. If the church leaders feel like this is an attack on them it is not but it is the truth.

Our heavenly father and the king of us all, he created everyone and everything and he has given us all a free will and 2 timothy 1:7 says "for god hath not given us the spirit of fear; but of power; and of love, and of a sound mind". Power over evil, power over the sin, power over the mind and body and power or dominion over the earth. Love is so that we can give to one another and to love one another and love is respecting one another's free will that God has given to all of us and a sound mind is for us to make honest and fair and logical decisions for ourselves.

The people put the government in power to make these decisions, the same people in your church might I add. If they wanted the church to run the country and to make these decisions, then they would have put the leader of the churches in power, am I right or wrong? Think about it for a minute, nowhere was I personally fixing the churches and please do not say what does fixing the church have to do with me? It is not just you or me it is all of us and the leaders of the churches need to address this, mainly them because they are the leaders.

You might say, okay here we go fixing the churches. I know we must put God first!!! You might say God is first in my church but think about what is going on in your church, the good the bad and the ugly. The church is supposed to be a place of righteousness, of prayer and worshiping God, and anything that is not righteous is bad and does not belong in the churches. I know you know that, so why are they not doing godly things, like going out in the communities and helping poor people and seeing what they can do for the people in the communities and bringing the people back to together. I feel as if the church has the key and the power to bring the flock back to the church once the church stops being so divided. The church needs to come back together because it's seems like every pastor, priest, bishop, prophet and minster wants their church to succeed but something is missing. I could go on all day about the churches falling by the way side but I have to move on but before I do let me just say this, we all need to take responsibility for our actions whether it's the person, the church, the police or the government. No man is perfect on earth, but Jesus was and Jesus said "be ye perfect for your heavenly father is perfect". Jesus said "be" as in becoming perfect, so if Jesus said we can become perfect then we can do it with God's love and guidance.

LAWS THAT NEED TO BE CHANGED

Do you think that change is something that can be avoided? I say no, and if you think about it you will say no too!!! So why are we not embracing it, the time is long overdue and it seems to me like we are the only ones that are not making any changes or headway in the country. One of the most necessary changes that needs to be made is the changing and modernizing of the countries outdated laws that don't reflect the changing times in the Bahamas.

The days of bondage are long gone. I know we have some people who wish those days were still around so that they can have more power over the poor people with outdated laws. Change is one thing that you can be sure that is going to happen and the man or woman who ushers in good changes their name will echo in the minds of Bahamians until the end of days. All good things are from God, and how do you know if something is good or righteous? You know when it benefits everybody in a righteous way even if that person does not want it or like it. For example God gives all of his children eternal life, but a lot of us do not want it or do not want to do what it takes get it.

But let me say this may God bless the man or woman that brings in good change to the Bahamas and its people. I will also say may good change rain from Long Island to Eight Mile Rock to the vast land of Andros and

PROGRESS

to the pink sanded beaches of Eleuthera. This is a quote from {Dr. Martin Luther King Jr.} may God bless his soul.

In order to know what laws are out dated and needs to be changed, the easiest thing to do would be to talk to the people, have town meetings so you can hear what the people have to say and that will let them know that they are a big part of the Bahamas and its law making. Without the people the Bahamas would be just another island, and the laws are for the people in the country so why shouldn't they have some say in what laws are good for them or not. The lawyers and the law firms need to be a part of this also, because who better than lawyers that can tell you which laws need to be charged and have become redundant. Let them put there five cent in because they practice the law every day and know more about the law then a lot of us and they can see the holes in the system.

There are a few laws that I see that are necessary and need to be implemented in the country, firstly a self-defense law to protect the person who is being attacked by a group of persons or by one particular person because many times I have seen a group of men attacking this one person because they feel untouchable in a large group, or because one person in the group does not like that one person or because they want what that one person has. When the police comes to the scene they would lockup that one person who is being attacked regardless of what that one person did or didn't do. That person has a right to protect and defend themselves and it's not for that group of people to decide whether or not he or she is guilty or not because that is for the counts to decide so please let us look at implementing a self-defense law.

The next one is that everybody must have two forms of government Identification beside their passport and one of them must be on that person at all times, like a drivers license or a voters card that looks like a driver licenses. Young people eighteen and under should have a school I.D that is given to them by the government with the government seal on it. It should have information about the school that they attend and other information on it so that we can keep track of our kids and know who they are and what they are doing. The reason why this is so important is because when the police are questioning someone on the street and that person doesn't have any identification on them they could say that they are so and so and tell the police anything. If that person is wanted for a crime but he does not have any identification on him then the police would not know for sure who that person is, just this reason alone is good enough to make this the law. It is important that everybody has a Bahamian identification on them at all times and not just some of the people but everybody ten years and older Bahamian and non Bahamian alike. If the U.S can do it with their three hundred million people I am sure we can do it with our three hundred and fifty thousand people, and the Bahamian flag will not be desecrated by anyone.

Here are a few more laws that need to implemented. No one under the age of twenty one should be able to buy or drink alcohol because of the simple reason that it is a drug albeit a legal drug but it is still a drug. Every country in the world that allows their people to drink alcohol in public could testify to this and they have tons of evidence to back up testimony that alcohol is a deadly substance in the wrong hands. With this law I propose that if you are found with alcohol and you are under twenty one you and the person or bar that you got it from will be charged with a crime and you will be fined or do jail time. The bars that sell alcohol to under age people will be fined heavier than the underage person who buys the alcohol.

No one under the age of twenty one should be allowed to work in bars because alcohol is not for kids and people who are not responsible people. To have a few drinks of any kind of alcohol is a privilege given by law and not a right given by birth so no one under the age of twenty one should be allowed in to be in night clubs either. These things are privileges, so in the meantime those kids that are eighteen to twenty they could learn about responsibly and how to use good judgment and to have respect for these things because they are in the real world. We should teach them and protect them from themselves because this world does not care about them and will walk all over them. They are the future of the Bahamas and besides they have too many things to do like looking for a job, getting in to a college and finding a career so that they can become productive citizens of the Bahamas.

Chapter Two

THE ECONOMY OF THE BAHAMAS

The Bahamas economy is in one big mess; yeah I said it, what a mess. Picture this, you take your bucket to the pump to get water and as soon as you start filling it with water the bucket starts leaking from everywhere, you have already wasted your time going to the pump just to find out the bucket has holes in it that you can't see. Let me tell you what I mean when I say this, the bucket is the country and the water is the money and wasting time is you working hard to live in a better country but there is not enough water to improve and make the country better because the money keeps going right back out of the county.

One of the goals of the Bahamas should be to become financially stable but how can we become financially stable if the bucket is leaking water like crazy because the more water we put in the bucket the more water will come out of the bucket and as obvious as that is the people in charge can't see this. Now between me and you, you know that does not make any sense, that is like a dog chasing his tail, "stupid". We need the right people to get in there and patch those holes in the bucket and save as much water as we can.

What makes an economy strong is poor and middle class people spending money and the money goes into small businesses and then in the bucket and back in to the people's hands and homes, and the money goes round and round and up and down from front to back and hand to hand rather than the money leaving the country. In the first chapter of this book I showed you where there is untouched money in the county.

See the problem is not that the people in the county aren't spending money, but the true problem is that the money is running out of the bucket or the country. Let me point out something that I feel that needs to be changed in this economy and why the water keeps coming out of the bucket.

(1) The tourism industry has serviced us very well this far, but we can't keep depending on it to sustain our economy. We know that after September 11th and the last two years the county has been in a deep recession and not because of Bahamians. God forbid that we have another September 11th. I'm not saying we should push the tourism industry aside, I'm just saying that it should not be our number one industry any more, maybe number three, and sure, the money that comes in from the tourism industry we will be glad to accept that too and add that to the pot or to the bucket or to the treasury any one of these you prefer.

So what should be our number one industry that we should pay a lot of attention to? The economy, in the first charter of this book I showed you how we can get money from income and company taxes. Let's review this idea, income tax will bring in a year about $165 million a year and that is the minimum from what I calculated for that chapter, the company tax is about $20 million minimum into the bucket or the treasury each year then add that with the two hundred million dollars from tourism, see this is just an example and that's only three places to get sure money from. The fourth one would be customs duties that are another two hundred million minimum, just in these four industries alone the minimum I came up with is $558 million dollars a year even though it will be more than that. Now think of how much more money there is to be collected in the country.

There is another way we can stop the water from coming out of the bucket, by making things cheaper in the country to buy because we still have a lot of people who are still going away to buy food and clothes and other items that they can get right here at home. The things we have locally are just as good as the stuff over in the U.S, but some people think that it is better over there. I would say just better price at times and better deals on stuff but not better quality. As a case in point, ten to fifteen years ago contractors and builders would go and buy all of their building stuff for their project that they are working on from the U.S. This does not always make much sense to do that's because the prices are just as good at home. If you don't believe me then check around to different building supply stores. If we make the products cheaper at home for the people, they would spend their money at home rather than spending more money to go to the US to shop. When people shop at home rather than away that means more business for the mom and pops stores and the big stores alike, and the more sales the businesses make the more people they will need to work and the more people getting hired, the more people that are working, and the more money is being spent and remaining in the country. I ask you again am I right or wrong?

I know what you might be saying how can we stop people from bringing in whatever they want in the country? It's simple; we don't have to stop them if they want to bring in something and it is less expensive in the country, that is up to them if they want to waste their money.

Let me give you a clear picture of what I'm talking about, let's say grocery or food has a 50% duty on all food products that is imported into the country and the government put the duty up to 70% for anyone who is bringing food products. For big stores and the moms and pops stores they drop the duty to 40%, now you tell me would you bring in a box of chicken for $150.00 and you can get it at home for $105.00? I know what you would do because I would do the same thing too, save me some money. The government would not be losing that much money and they would make it back in the amount of stuff that is being brought into the country and at the same time making it better for the people and building a strong economy.

You might like this idea, if I was the leader of the country I would have borrowed twenty billion dollars from that country who likes the Bahamas (China) and who are giving us millions and millions of dollars in gifts. I know what you are thinking, well it's a good thing that you are not the Prime Minister of the country because borrowing that amount of money is going to put us deeper in debt and how are we going to pay it back when we can't pay of the bills we have now? Indeed, I will show you how we can pay all of our old bills off and turn over all that money. I am sure they would lend us the money, it may take some time but we would get it, and before you say anything let me tell you how I would spend this twenty billion in the country.

Let us move pass the agreements and the paper work and go right to receiving of the next fifty years or maybe even sooner than that. The first thing I would do with the money is to take ten billion of that money and lock it in a high interest rate account with no risk (when I say me I mean me and the house of parliament and remember now in this example I am the Prime Minster of the country or the one who is leading the country) and this money in this account will be for national disasters or if we have to jump start the Bahamas economy again one day. The only way any one can get their hands on this money is by 98% of the house of parliament approving it, even if we get 1% interest minimum on this ten billion dollars a year, one hundred million dollars a year minimum interest is a lot to me I could live off of that for rest of my life and my kids and their kids.

The next thing I would do is to pay off all of government outstanding loans, that amounts to about 1.5 billion dollars if it is that much or it may be more than that, this is just a number that I came up. Moving on that will leaver 8.5 billion dollars, of which we the government will put two billion into the treasury to take care of every day government affairs. Bear in mind I did not say, me the leader or the other members of parliament should get a pay increase, that leaves 6.5 billion dollars in a different government account.

I would give money to start the farming industry on a large and vast scale in the country, so big that we are able to feed ourselves and export to other Caribbean countries and I would get everybody in the country involved even if they are only buying or selling what the famers grow. I must say that I don't know what the cost or price is going to be to do this but I'm thinking about one billion dollars. I ask again, what do you think? Think about what a large farming industry would do for us because everybody has to eat.

That still leaves five billion five hundred million dollars, so then we would put some money back in the tourism product like building the things and creating the environment that we know that the tourist would love to be in and would have lots of fun in. This is not just in Nassau but as many of the islands as possible. Each island should have two or three major docks for fishing boats and big and small yachts alike, not including the dock for the mail boats. The docks should also have yacht clubs in walking distance and build around the yacht club vacation homes and time sharing condos. We should create a wonderful environment that is truly the Bahamas and true to our culture.

We need to have at least two places like Sandy Port or Old Fort Bay on each island where people with money can just park their boats right in the back of their yard and everyday people could live there also. If you ask anyone they would tell you that they would love to be able to park a nice boat in the back of their yard on the water, men and women alike. We can do this by ourselves or bring in investors to partner up with the government to achieve this goal just like what they are doing with the new airport. The lots going on sale for Bahamians and non-Bahamian alike will be a part of this beautiful environment to come. This should run us into about one and a half billion dollars.

After all of that we are still left with about four billion dollars to improve the country and its people. The next thing I would do is I would have a meeting with all three of those entities that have been here for a very long time, when I say a long time I mean a long time, ones that have been here for 100 hundred years or 75 years and the others I cannot really say but I know that they were doing some good business in the country. The meeting would be to let them know how much we appreciate them for supporting us and helping us build our country throughout the decades and that we would like to continue doing business with them, but we as a country cannot keep doing business the same way for the next fifty or hundred years.

The time has come for us to change things for the better and for the people, the economy and the country. I would say this to these entities that the day will come when I will ask the same of other entities in the country. I believe if you want to change something you have to deal with the big fish first. I would say to them that we the government of the Bahamas and the people would like it if you would sell forty percent of your company shares or stocks to the Bahamian people so that they can own apart of their future. I know there would be a lot of resistance from one or two of them maybe even all three of them, but that is to be expected. That aside do you know how much money these entities pay out to their shareholders a year in dividends? If the company here in the Bahamas is worth 1.5 billion dollars then you tell me what you think the shareholder is paid out in a year? Bahamians have almost no shares in these entities; it's time for that to change. I feel it is far pass the time for that to change. Can you think of the amount of money that they have paid out to their shareholders over all these years? I think it is in the hundreds of millions if not billions of dollars. Please tell me if these foreign companies are making this kind of money off of our economy and us, why can't Bahamians be a part and own a part of these money making entities.

Now I know that two of them are Canadian companies, but if they decide not to sell shares to the Bahamians then we would have to buy them out. I would say no less than ninety percent of each company, with the other four billion dollars that we still have left that we borrowed from our friends. Can you image you owning shares in a billion dollar company and how much money you would get when it is time for profit sharing.

PROGRESS

Think about it, you will do all your business at this company just because you have shares in these companies which also means the Bahamas economy and stock market will become even stronger and they will need to hire more people.

So we might be left with three to five hundred million dollars give or take, so then we move on to the roads and airport on the islands that are in bad shape, the roads need to be paved from one end of the island to the next end from front to back and the airports, the more south you go the airports gets worst.

I know we would be able to do unlimited things with that type of money; we could even start the new city in Andros the one I talked about in this book. When I say unlimited, I mean unlimited, this is like planting billions and billions of seeds and waiting for the crop to grow so it can be harvested. Think about it? What would you do if you were the Prime Minister and you had ten billion dollars to spend on the country to bring it back to paradise?

Before I forget, can we please put some money into Potters Cay dock, the road needs to be opened up some more, and all the vendors stalls need to be built over and painted with Bahamians colors. The bathrooms also need to be fixed and painted and they also need about two more new bathrooms. All of the old boats out there they need to be removed and their needs to be a law that if you can't keep your boat looking good and pained it must be moved. The police station should also be moved to a new location as there is an empty lot to the right of Domino's pizza right across from the dock, that is a good location for a police station in my opinion. Next we need to build the fruit vendors better stalls and all of the vendors need to have running water and government power and the staff that work for these food vendors must take a course on how to service the public and their customers. I hate when I go to have lunch out by the dock or anywhere in the Bahamas or anywhere in the world and the staff have bad attitudes. We need to fix this please if we want our tourism product to last, and if I were a tourist I would not go to a place that looks like that or even think about eating from there at the dock. This is just my opinion about Potters Cay dock because if I'm in Paradise I should be eating from a place that looks more like paradise.

Here is another concern that I have. There are about nine different water companies and half of them sell some very good drinking water. I am sure you know what I mean because you may drink their water and maybe their juice. With all of these companies in the Bahamas, why are we still importing bottled drinking water from out of the county? That doesn't make any sense at all to me. There are enough water bottling companies to supply Nassau and the family islands with bottled water. What would this mean if we stop bottled water from coming in to the country? It would mean more business for the water companies, so they would need more employees to work for them, and the money that was spent on non-Bahamian bottled water would stay in the country.

The same thing could be done with the chicken farm in Abaco and not just chicken but any live stock that we grow here in the Bahamas. There are only three things these businessmen and farmers would need and that would be the government financial support and the support of the people in the country. We could also do this with the companies that make windows and doors and the ones that make beds and mattress or any company that manufactures any product in the Bahamas.

It is little small things like this that makes the economy function properly and keep money in circulation. It also helps the little business that keep people working just like the little heart in your body that keeps the blood in your body going round and round in your body.

The government is in the middle of signing many tax information treaties with many different countries, and I know we need to sign them so we can stay off the blacklist for countries that are called tax havens. My hope is that in these treaties the government is looking out for the best interest of the country and its people first because the other countries would come and take the bread right out of our mouths if we let them. You may ask what does this have to do with the Bahamas economy?

Ok let's look at this, if I was the head of the government I would have made sure to put legislation in these treaties that stipulate that if a non-Bahamian wanted to put his or her money in a bank in the

Bahamas and he or she does not want to be taxed by their country or don't want their government to know about their money in the Bahamas, that non Bahamas would have to become a citizens of the Bahamas and they must live here in the Bahamas for at least six months out of the year and they must give up all rights of citizenship to any other country. They would have to obtain a Bahamian passport and they would have to declare their total net worth to the Bahamas government. They must also keep the liquid cash here in the Bahamas and they will be taxed 1% on their money and that will be their income tax to the government. By doing it this way no other country would have any jurisdiction over that person or their money or whatever they have in the Bahamas. The other country would only be able to tax them on whatever they have in that country, like a house or land or a company.

I think this would be safeguarding our economy and here is why!! If that person has let's say ten million dollars that they are bringing with them to this country and we charge them 1% income tax on that ten million dollars that would be one hundred thousand dollars a year in income tax that would be paid to the government.

I do not think that they would have a problem with this because if we compare what they are being taxed now on their money in their country it would be far more than 1%. From the interest alone on their money they would be able to pay this 1% with no problem and even if that person only has one hundred thousand dollars that will still be a good thing for the government to receive a thousand dollars a year in income tax from them. That person would then want to buy a house and a car and maybe open a business and that would mean more jobs for Bahamians and more money in the economy. With this thought in mind, if you were the leader of the country would you or would not put a piece of legislation like this in the treaties so that we would not be left out in the cold without proper safeguards. I think this will help us in safeguarding ourselves, our economy and our future.

I have noticed that there is a company that is buying up small companies and building one very large company. I personally do not see anything wrong with that to a point because we don't have any laws that I am aware of that would stop companies from cornering the market or buying up all the companies that are in the same field. Right now it is almost free reign once the financial backing is there. My only problem with this is the fact that the Bahamian people don't have ownership of at least 40% of this company. It is good that the company is continually growing and it has Bahamian owners but I am not sure how many non-Bahamians own stock in this company. To my knowledge the Bahamian person who owns this company also owns about three or four medical facilities around town that works hand and hand with their larger company. I am always happy when a Bahamian is doing what the government isn't or can't do right now and I wish them all the best.

What I do not like with some entities and individuals is the attitude of all for me, persons who want everything for themselves and their family and friends and not sharing with other Bahamians. They get on my nerves sometimes but we are all one people and one Bahamas, one love and one country, so with that said it would be good if that person or persons would put at leases 40% of the company's stock on the market for Bahamians so they could be a part of this growing company. I think it's much better this way because it will insure that Bahamians own a part of their future. I am not just talking about private companies but also such entities as the three government companies, namely B.T.C, B.E.C and W & S. If this is done I would want you to sit back and watch how much good will come from this once it is done right. All I am asking for is that it be done and done the right way.

Here is another hole in the bucket that I think if we close it up it will do a lot of good for the people of this country and the economy. I am referring to a national medical health care plan. I believe this is very easy to do since we are only three to four hundred thousand strong in the country. That makes it even easier to implement. Of course we would need to know how to put it together or build it for the people.

Here is what I would do if I were in charge. I would bring all of the C.E.O'S of the companies that carry medical health insurance plans together and tell them that we need a national medical insurance plan for the country. I have one in mind that would work like this;

first of all we would create a new insurance company just for medical insurance and all of the insurance companies that are at this meeting would have shares in this company along with the government and the people of the Bahamas. We would then take all of the people who have medical insurance with these companies and put them into this new company and then I would ask the insurance companies to drop the rates lower and be more cost effective. The government along with the National Insurance Board would back this company and have shares in this company and inform the people that this is what we came up with for the national health insurance plan. We will point out that the government cannot afford to do this on its own and pay the whole bill.

Once this is done we would drop the price for insurance for men from $150.00 to $ 90.00 and for women from $200.00 to around $110.00. Children would begin at $27.50 for girls until they reach five years old and then every five years it will increase by $27.50 or thereabouts so that by the time the girls are twenty one the rates would be the same as adult female rates. This could go up to about $125.00 depending on how healthy the female is. The same would be done for the boys also and if the men do put this company together and make this happen I want to be a big part of it, after all it is my idea.

If the national health plan is done this way it will be cheaper for people to afford health insurance. If only 75% of the people in the country were to join this medical insurance plan that would mean better rates for the people and more business for this new insurance company and more jobs for Bahamians. Let us face it, all of us are not sick at one time and not even half of us will be sick at the same time. It stands to reason then that if all of us in the Bahamas, or let us say 90% of us were to join this medical insurance plan who knows, we may even be able to get the rates down to a lower price for every man, woman, girl and boy in the country.

We will never know what the possibilities are unless we put this in place. With the government backing this company and making sure that there is no foolishness going on, the insurance companies will not be able to run over the people. How can we lose? Please correct me if I am wrong. Almost all of the insurance companies buy insurance from larger insurance companies outside this country. If that is the case then the government needs to open up a new branch so that all of the insurance companies can buy coverage from this government. Let us remember that the government has over ten billion dollars on a fixed deposit account which is more than enough to serve as a reserve against losses. This would mean rather than buying insurance from somewhere else they would spend and keep the money at home. In addition there is more to this medical insurance health plan that I will continue to outline.

Do you have any idea how much good this could do for this country and its people and the economy? Let me tell you, all of the private medical institutions like the heart doctors, the eye doctors, the brain doctors, the skin doctors, dentists' gynecologists, pediatrician doctors and so forth. All of these doctors will be able to take the medical insurance card which would mean that they would need to hire more people to work for them and they will need more equipment. This would create more opportunity for Bahamians to advance in the medical field. They may be able to open their own private clinic or pharmacies and anything having to do with medical insurance we will need more of. By doing this, it would clearly show that the private insurance companies are more than ready for growth and change in the country.

One of the holes in the bucket that I talked about earlier in this book is making numbers legal. The Prime Minister has said himself if the government were to legalize the numbers game it would bring in about fifty million dollars in taxes in to the treasury a year so we need to stop wasting time and just do what it takes and get it done and call it a day.

When the economy is doing well and people can work and take home a good paycheck at the end of the week it makes them feel good about themselves and I am sure it will have a positive impact on the crime rate. A country without a vision for the future is one that is lost at sea in the dark. The good part about this is that it is in our hands and we can make the changes, making it better for ourselves. I believe all of us would want to make it better for our families. God did not create the recession; man did in order to shift the money and power to their side.

The figures that I came up with so far in this book are not one hundred percent right so you can work your own numbers and compare. I believe we should try this before dismissing the idea. With the plan I outlined, there are one hundred thousand men and women in the medical insurance plan and they are paying one hundred dollars a month. If you multiply that by one hundred thousand, and then multiply that by twelve months, tell me what amount you would come up with? Which company in the Bahamas would not be able make it off of this kind of money. This is my original idea and it belongs to me.

Let me point out a few other things, if I was in charge of the government I would make it illegal for people to write bad checks. They know that they do not have any money in their checking account so that would be stealing and stealing is against the law right? Why not make it against the law and put in tough penalties for those lying and stealing people. If I do not have the money on my checking account then I would not write the check.

January 10th is called majority rule day and I know most of us know what that means. I think the government should put in a "Shut the hell up day" in the law for those people who do not add anything to the cause or who do not bring any ideas and solutions and only bring their negative views to the table. These people stop progress and if one man has an idea or a solution to fix a problem and no one else has another idea to fix the problem they would reject the idea because of who the person is. In cases like this I believe the person who has the idea should have the right to be able to say, "shut the hell up!" because you did not come up with any other solutions for the problem.

Remember that old saying, you can lead a horse to water but you cannot make the horse drink, all of these ideas and views that I've pointed out are mine and only to be used by permission. The bible says, God gave us richly all things (not to love) to enjoy through his son Jesus Christ. So what are we waiting on?

THE NEW AIRPORT & HOSPITAL

I was going to give the authorities an ear full about the deplorable condition of the Nassau international Airport but by the time I got to this part of the book they had already beat me to the deal. The new airport is now finished and looking pretty good I must say. From the looks of it I would say it was worth the wait. I must say to all of those persons who were responsible for the new airport from start to finish and especially those making sure that it is done correctly, good work, and the same to you to Mr. Prime Minster for ensuring that this project was completed.

That being said let us not forget about the other airports on the Family Islands that need to be renovated. Before I leave the Nassau airport alone, let me point out something, if the airport is named after the father of the nation then let us show him some respect and give the airport the right name, his name is Sir Lynden Pindling and the airport should be the Sir Linden Pindling international airport not Lynden Pindling airport. We need to remember in this country that RESPECT is not dead. Many people push it aside or don't know what it is to have respect or to give respect but respect is always needed and needs to be given at all times, so let's respect and honor him in the right way always.

Let me say this also, let us not forget how he brought us this far regardless if you are P.L.P or F.N.M, I know everybody would like to be respected honored and remembered for their 25 years of hard work and dedication to Bahamas and its people.

The man or woman who says that they don't want to be remembered for their good and hard work in this country I would say something must be wrong with their head. I am sure that the other two leaders (who have served as Prime Minister) would want us to respect honor and remember them in the right ways because without the first there could not have been a second and third. It is my conviction therefore that his proper and full name SIR Linden Oscar Pindling should be what appears on the Airport, thank you.

THE NEW HOSPITAL

I hear talk about a new hospital once or twice every blue moon, the new hospital that we need so desperately because we have out grown the Princess Margaret Hospital since the 1990's. This hospital is deplorable but that is what the poor people have to deal with. I guess the leaders can say there is no money to build a new hospital right now and I would agree with them on that but only until a year after this book has been published and in the public's hands I believe it will give the governing party a clear picture on how to make money in order to build this new hospital. As I have said before you can only lead a horse to water but you cannot make him drink it.

I personally think the new hospital should cost about three to five hundred million dollars and that should be an excellent one for that price that will last for a very long time and support the needs of the growing population in the Bahamas.

I foresee the location of the new hospital being on Thompson Boulevard on the side of the new building next to the Ministry of Public Works. I think that is the perfect location because it is easy to get to from the south the west and the northwest and almost all of the highways that run south west and north lead right in to this area. For the eastern side of town the Doctors Hospital will service that area. I know at the moment not everybody can afford Doctors Hospital, but if the insurance companies come to together like I mentioned to you about the medical insurance plan then almost everybody would be able to afford to see a private doctors or go to the hospital.

Now you see that it is as easy as one before two and two before three, one two three or A B C anyone you prefer.

Now what should we expect from this new hospital, I see a building that is ten to fifteen floors high with two or three wings, lots of parking, a powerful backup generator that can run the whole hospital and air conditioning from top to the bottom. It would also have a daycare center for the staff kids and for the people who are visiting the sick. This hospital should have a chapel for people to come and pray and state of art medical equipment, fiber optic cable, impact windows and doors, new ambulances about five new ones and an air ambulance like a helicopter. The hospital should have state of the art operating rooms, recovery rooms, an excellent children's ward and a well-equipped cancer ward. The doctors and the nurses would also need good areas for them to change, shower and sleep.

I am not trying to tell them how to build this new hospital but I am just saying this is what we should be looking forward to. If we are going to spend hundreds of millions of dollars to build a new hospital we better do it the right way and not half way. This new hospital will require more office staff, more nurses, more doctors, more orderlies and security and that means more Bahamians having jobs.

Now I know what you might be thinking? How is this new hospital going to make money? If the government were to implement the medical health insurance plan that I recommended previously in this book then people would be able to pay their bills. Examine the facts and tell me if I am right or wrong? The next question would be? How would the government be able to pay a big staff like this in the new hospital? When people are able to pay their bills on time then the hospital is making money and can pay their staff and the staff is able to pay income tax and see how the money goes round and round and it all falls in line.

Why do we need a big hospital like this? Because this new hospital is not only for today or next year it is for the future of the Bahamas and its growing population. The Bahamas will see the population grow to a million people one day so I say let's be ready.

REGULATING LAWYERS, DOCTORS, BANKERS, CONTRACTORS AND INSURANCE COMPANIES.

We must regulate lawyers. It would be the understatement of the year that lawyers run this county. Just take a look at the house of parliament, it is filled with lawyers. I did not write this chapter to say anything bad about them even though some of them deserve it and I know that there is the bar association to keep them in line but somehow they always seem to get around poor people and abuse them. All that I am saying is we need tougher rules for them. Just because they practice the law and they know how to get around it, does that mean they can consistently break the law? I'm not talking about all of them just a hand full of them and no one should have free reign not even lawyers should have free rein to break the law. There are dishonest lawyers just like there are dishonest police officers as I talked about earlier in this book.

You have some lawyers that think that they are doing the poor people some big favor, they need to check themselves because if I am paying you to do a job then that is not a favor (I am sure that they know that because they went to law school). If what I am saying offends you then you must be one of these lawyers that I am talking about. At one time I had a lawyer and she was with me for about five years. I was doing some good business with her and the law firm that she worked for every year for five years until it came to a very, very important matter that she was in charge of and should have taken care of for me. She sat back and did nothing, she started it, and that was about it, the matter was in limbo for eight months, I then reported her to her bosses, and I do not know what happened with her because they never got back to me, but my point is, if you start something finish it, if you broke something you fix it and take responsibility for your actions or in her case her lack of action. If she is reading this I don't care if she gets mad or not, just do the job that you are being paid to do. I never asked for any favors only that you do the work that I'm paying you for. This is not high school anymore, this is the real world and if you want to run with the big boys then you have to do or put in the hard work and dedication that is required. After five years I have no idea what when wrong with her, it may have been a personal issue, who knows? Only her one can say what went wrong, but whatever it was it still should not have affected my business or her work. A small word like sorry can fix the biggies problems, but the truth is the truth, accept it so you can be at peace with yourself. This was to prove my case and point and not to offend any of the good lawyers or any of the law firms.

It is all of these little things that can contribute to the corruption and down fall of society. One day it is going to cause a collapse of the pillars of the justice system because we are not fixing it and it is slowly eating away at the system and one day the system will not be able to bare the load.

To be a doctor is indeed a noble profession and it is a profession that will always be respected but you have some doctors that still need to be supervised and regulated. As case in point I remember when a junior doctor operated on a woman about four or five years ago and this doctor butchered this woman's stomach. She is still alive that I am aware of but her and her husband sued the Princess Margaret hospital and they settled the case out of court. I still do not believe that the case has been satisfied or the money has been paid to them as yet and there have been hundreds of cases like this over the years consistently happening in this country where they leave operating tools inside of people or misdiagnosis and improper treatment remains to be seen. We know that doctors have a big responsibility to take care of the people and I must say we love and appreciate all of the doctors but they still need to be regulated. Just like a good son he may be a good boy and does his work and does what you tell him to do but he still needs rules to govern him. In the same way doctors may be good doctors but they still need rules to be governed by, as well as many other professionals including bankers and contractors.

I know for sure that there are a lot of people who would have a lot to say about contractors in this town. I know about some of them and the rest of them I have heard of, the okay and good contractors know that there are bad contractors out there that are giving them a bad name. Some of them are not showing up for the job and they already have your money while others are doing bad work and half assed work and over charging for the job.

When they steal your money the only thing or the right thing that you could do is take them to court in hopes of getting your money back. In fact I am dealing with a case like this now in court after two and a half years of going to court and winning the case I still have not received my money. I still have to go back to court to see if the judge will make the contractor pay me my money after two and half years, this does not make any damn sense. That is too long to be waiting for something that belongs to me. If I was waiting on that money to finish my house I would have still been up the river without paddles, no way in the world should a little case like that take so long.

Does anybody out there watch Judge Judy? I am sure she would have had this case settled immediately. Listening to this the judge made me pay the contractors lawyer for coming to court to represent him. I know what you are thinking, that judge cannot be in his right mind. I cannot believe it myself, the only thing a case like this is doing is blocking up the court system. Let's get it together people it should not take this long or be this way where the bad contractor gets your money in their pockets in one day and its takes two years for you to get your money back from him through the courts system and when the court tells him to pay you back it's in small amounts each month. Between the bad contractors, the bad plumbers and the bad electricians, take it from me, do not give them your money up front and let them tell you what to buy and when the work is finished. You should check the work yourself and make sure it is finished and how you want it before paying them the balance. I would say do not even give them half up front, let them work first and then get paid because you worked for your money first and then you got paid. This is the best way for it to be because in this current system you can't win for losing, so make them work first and then they get paid.

Now to the insurances companies, I could go on all day about the things they have done and still do to poor people. The one thing I will say is we need a lot more rules regulations and fines for them because some of them think that they are untouchable. Imagine what would happen if the government took my idea into consideration for the national health insurance plan, we would definitely need them to be regulated even more and that's my five cents on that.

ILLEGAL IMMIGRANT PROBLEM

This is a vexing problem and if I was in charge I would have made it a law that an illegal immigrant would work until they have made enough money to pay for their plane ticket back to where ever they are from. It may sound cold but something must be done, and remember now, they are breaking our laws when they come here illegally, so it is in the government's best interest to do what is necessary to contain this problem because it's slowly getting out of hand.

From what I can see the government is doing what they can about the problem, and almost all of us has had a Haitian working for us and yes they are looking and need a better way of life. I can't give them wrong for that because if it was me or you we would have done the same thing too. In spite of this we the Bahamas cannot take that on, it is another countries problem that has become our own.

If five percent of Haitians come here from Haiti this Bahamas would sink. Picture this, there are five people in your little boat and the boat can only hold eight people but there are fifty people in the water that need help what would you do? Try to save them? Or save the people in your boat? I know your answer, but this is what we are faced with.

RESPECT

Respect is a word that you don't hear about now a days, it is also one of my favorite words that defines me and its right up there with progress. Like I said earlier, respect is not dead and it didn't leave the country it is right here. Respect and being respectful should always be relevant. The way you walk, the way you talk and the way you act, should be based upon respect but the people in this country just don't seem to care about respect anymore. Their attitude is often like, "the hell with respect", but they want you to have and give them respect and who says that they deserve it?

Here is what the dictionary has to say about respect, "to show consideration for, a willingness to obey, or thoughtfulness, to show or feel admiration for, to give a good opinion of." Here is what respect should mean for Bahamians, Self Respect: means to hold yourself in high regard or a sense of self worth or in other words, you mean a lot to yourself. Respecting Others: it means to give respect to others without others having to give you something or doing something for your respect, and not having something to say about a person that you can't respectfully say to their face.

Respect Others Property: when you get your new car that you spend 20 to 30 thousand dollars for and someone comes and flats the tires or put a mark on the car that you have to pay to get fixed, that's not respecting other people's property. Respecting other people's property is showing consideration for someone else's things that is not yours because you would want that person to take care of your property because it means a lot to you.

General Respect: is respecting people places and things, respecting those two persons that brought you into this world even if they are not a part of your life, respect the fact that they gave you life. Respect that old man or woman that cussed you out, for the simple reason that they are old enough to be your mother or father and they were alive longer than you, even though it may not seem fair that you show respect and say nothing and walk away. Respect for the police is another issue. The other night I went to get me something to eat around 2 am in the morning and I left my car keys in the car and the police came and told me about doing that and not to do it again because it was cause unnecessary work for them. I agreed with him and I said to the police officer you are right and as he was leaving and I said to him have a good night officer and he said ok and you have a good night too. Now that is respect.

Respect for other peoples relationship and respecting one another in the relationship. I know when you have that person you want in your life it feels so good and so right and you don't want anyone to interfere with that, right? You want them to respect the fact that you are with that person, right? Well, just give others the same respect for their relationships, it's that simple. Respect your relationship: like not giving yourself to another person when you are in a relationship and not doing things you don't want your boyfriend or girlfriend to do to you. Respecting other people's space, it is an unwritten law that you have to respect other people's space whether you like it or not because you would want them to respect your space and it's as simple as that.

Respecting places: is respecting the places that you go to, like if you visit a person or friend or family members house you should respect their place and act like you are use to something even if you are not used to having a place to call your own. Respect is the key, and when you are in Rome do as the Romans do. I said that to say when you go to another man's country you should follow their rules, by that i mean showing respect for places. Respecting other people's place is to keep it in good conduction and not to destroy what does not belong to you.

You see in this life there are some things that you need to have to go along with integrity such as accepting the wonderful love of God and his glory through his son Jesus Christ our lord and savior, then there is self-respect, respecting others, brotherly love and kindness. These are the things in life that help make a good person with integrity. Respect is the glue that holds a friendship together or a relationship, a partnership and a Marriage.

You know what really eats me alive is the fact that nobody talks about respect any more. You do not hear the leaders talk about it, you don't hear church ministers preach or talk about it on TV, it's not a topic in the schools but it should be. It doesn't appear that the police are trained with it or is it that a lot of them just don't care about respect (for the general public). People don't even talk about it, and the parents are not teaching their kids that manners and respect are the key to their character and it will help to open doors for them. It seems to be that there is a case of the no respect flu in this town and that's not a good thing.

Respect should be given freely without having to work for it because some people work all of their lives and still get no respect (such as in my opinion teachers, nurses etc.). Love and respect is one and the same and both should be given freely. Some people say you have to earn respect but that only applies to the job that you are doing, like you have to earn the other doctors respect or you will earn the other carpenters respect by the good work that you are doing. You also earn the boss's respect because you are a hard and honest worker. These are the times you should earn respect. Back in the day Bahamians had respect for one another and there wasn't much crime in the country, but nowadays a lot of Bahamians don't have respect for each other and now crime is out of hand so you tell me what's wrong with this picture? Talking about earning respect; did your mother and father tell you that you had to earn your food or the clothes on your back? No they gave these things to you freely, they did not have to but they did so you should show love and respect freely. You have been given freely all the good things of God so why are we holding these things back from one another?

Respect is to hold in high regard, and to care about is to show thoughtfulness and respect. As a case and point, when a woman loves a man she respects him whether or not she is in love with him. God loves and respects what he created so much that he gave us free will power and dominion over everything he created, (see genesis 1:26, 2 timothy 1:7). This is how deep love and respect goes and don't even try to deny this. We need to learn how to love respect and accept each other for who we are, even though some people make it very hard to give them respect because they don't know what respect is, or how to have respect for themselves (and then) or others

QUESTION: what does respect means to you?

MEN WOMEN & CHILDREN IN SOCIETY

Dear strong and beautiful women in society, we as men can't do this life without you; we can't have babies without you, we can't have a stable society without you, we can't teach our kids without you, we can't live a good life with you, and we can't rise up as men and stand tall without you. The wonderful love, kindness and beautiful spirit God has given women there is nothing else like it. We need you to take your rightful place in society right beside us, not as an adversary but as the matriarch of society.

We need you to teach our young women how to carry themselves, how to respect themselves and others and teach them the right way and the right things so they can do good things with their life and fear God. We need you to teach them to maintain the love, respect, integrity, good qualities and decency of a virtuous woman. We need you to teach them that everybody makes mistakes but you do not have to make the same mistake twice or a third time. If your boyfriend wants another child tell him you must be married so he can share the responsibly as a man and as a father. Teach them so it could be passed on to younger women and girls that are coming up in the Bahamas, let them know that their body belongs to them and they must take care of it and respect it because it has to last them all their life. We as men are calling on you for help, to help us keep our girls and boys in line and away from bad people, bad places and bad things and to show them what good people, good places and good things have to offer them.

With the love of God through his son Jesus Christ and having faith, we can and they (our kids) can achieve anything. Let them know that knowledge is the key that opens up the doors of opportunity and success, biblical knowledge, knowledge in school and in life because a person should never stop learning.

This is something I want you to all ways remember and you heard it here first. Oh my mother, Oh sister, Oh cousins, Oh my aunties I ask of you keep the ways of a virtuous woman as the women who were before you and passed virtue on to you, for proverbs: 31-10-31 clearly tells you of a virtuous woman. May love, peace, integrity, and respect be with you all the days of your life.

Oh men of the Bahamas where art thou? The boys of this day are running wild and being lead astray. We need your help oh good and strong men of society, help, help in the making of good boys that will become good men of society.

Help in the making of leaders, help in the home where the wife and kids are, help in changing the way society looks and thinks about young boys that are becoming men. Help "Oh" good men like Mr. Joseph Henry Rolle from D. W. Davis high school, a strong man that defines manhood we need many more like you.

Give oh men of society, give your time, give your heart, give the moneys that you can to help the boys that are lost and need to find their way back to God. Give brotherly kindness, give to them the love that God has given to you, and show them, and teach them the right ways in life for we were given power and dominion from the King in heaven over this world and our wife's and kids through his wonderful son Jesus Christ.

O men of society stop holding on to power, and teach the younger men how to take over and control power, for the man that has power only has power for a short time.

It is time we give our kids a sense of pride and belonging and direction because life has too many good things to offer to our children than for them to be partakers of the foolish things. Every child has the potential to become a good or great human being once we teach them the good things of God. Parents I know you remember this one, "wake up everybody no more sleeping in bed.... no more backward thinking time for thinking ahead..... The world has changed so very much from what it used to be..... There is so much hatred... war and poverty....... Wake up all you teachers time to teach them a new way.... maybe then they'll listen to what you have to say.... they're the ones who're coming up and the world is in their hands.... When you teach the children, teach them the very best you can...... the world won't get no better if we just let it be o no ,no, no, no; wake up everybody". {By teddy Pendergrass}

If that does not work beat (spank) their (kids) backsides from small, beat them until they blackout {I'm only joking about the blackout part} and then they will know who is in charge. Remember now kids are like sponges whatever you do they will suck that up and do that same thing or things (see Proverbs 13:24 and 19:18), for the best gift a father and mother can give their kids is wisdom and knowledge in my opinion, (see Proverbs 13:22 and 4:1-9 20-27) because in this life we only have the love of GOD and the gifts he has given us though his son Jesus Christ.

HONORING GREAT BAHAMAIN MEN & WOMEN

The people whose names that I am about to call are people who played monumental roles in the Bahamas and they made and help to make us what we are today. They brought us this far with their gifts, talents and their ability as leaders to stand strong and steadfast in the face of adversity. Let us honor them and never forget what they did for their country. I want to say Thanks to Mr. Leslie Miller and Mario's Bowling & Entertainment Center for keeping these persons names and their pictures and what they did for the Bahamas up on the wall in Mario's for people and younger ones to see, so that they would know who these persons are and what they did for the Bahamas. The names are in no particular order.

Let us start with the untouchable, SIR LYNDEN OSCAR PINDLING the father of the nation, born 1933 and died in 2000. Change started with him. Next is DAME MARGUERITE PINDLING, a strong beautiful and wonderful woman who supported her husband two hundred percent, we need a lot more women like you, SIR SIDNEY POITIER see all of his wonderful achievements on line or in his books, Rt. HON HUBERT A. INGRAHAM PM, Rt. HON PERRY G. CHRISTIE the former PM.

Archbishop Patrick c. Pinder St. Francis church, Dr. K.V.A. Rodgers medical field, Dr. Claudius Roland

Walker medical field, Mr. Charles W. Major Sr. sports, Dr. Francis Adderley medical field, Bishop Sam Green Zion united Baptist church, Dame Albertha Isaacs civil rights movement, Mr. Clarence Bain a true Bahamian, Mr. George Symonette music, Mr. Rick Fox sports, Mr. Wallace Groves the father of Freeport, Sir Milo Boughton Butler, Sir Gerald Cash, Sir Henry Taylor, Sir Orville Turnquest, Dame Ivy Dumont, Hon. Arthur D. Hanna, these are all the past governor generals of the Bahamas. Mr. Percival Vola Francis Junkanoo icon, Sir Randol Fawkes Government, Dr. Norman Gay medical field/ sports, Dr. Earle Farrington medical field, Mr. Danny Smith sports, Mr. Edward "Plunked" Taylor businessman, Rev. Tallmadge Sands Zion Baptist church, Mr. Freddie Munnings Sr, Entertainer, Mr. Paul Mcweeney banker, Canon William E. Thompson Anglican diocese, King Eric Gibson musical genius/Entertainer, Bishop Simeon Hall pastor/civil and social rights leader. Mr. Cecil Wallace Whitfield, Rev. Dr. Howard Brown, Sir Milo B. Butler, Dr. Doris Johnson, Sir Arthur D. Hanna, Mr. Clarence A. Bain, Sir Arthur

A. Foulkes, Dame Ivy Dumont education, Mr. G. Lightbourne, Mr. E. Pyfrom , Mr. R. Wilson, pioneer construction, Mr. Winston Saunders Attorney, Dr. Michael Symonette church, Dr. Timothy Barrett medical field, Sir Leonard Knowles the first chief justice, Bishop Rosten L. Davis The church, Tony "Obeah Man" McKay musical icon, Mrs. Margaret McDonald long career in government, Smokey 007 Leroy McKenzie musical icon, Mrs. Jane Bethel business woman, Mr. John Berkley "Peanuts" Taylor musical artist, Mr. Rupert Roberts business man, Bishop Michael Eldon The church, Mr. Elisha Obed boxing champion, Eugene Dupuch lawyer/ journalist /author/musician, Rev. Dr.

H.W Brown the church, Sir Jack Hayward G.B. port authority, Dr. Andrew Esfakis medical field, John Arthur Chippman "Chippie" performer, Sir Milo B. Butler a long and noble career in government, Mr. Ronnie Butler musical icon, Dr. Bernard Nottage medical field and government, Mr. Eddison Bethel broadcasting, Rev. Dr. Charles W. Saunders The church, Mr. James Catylyn poet /actor/director/producer/comedian, Mr. Leslie O. Miller sports/politician/business man, Dr. Elwood

Donaldson medical field/Politician, Pastor Tom Roberts The church, Rev. Dr. Ortland Bodie Sr., The church/ civil right, Mr. Franklyn Wilson business man /C.E.O of the Sunshine group, Professor Harry Edwards civil rights/sports, Ms. Maureen Duvalier cultural Icon, Mr. Mychal Thompson sports, Bishop Neil C. Ellis The church, Rev. Dr. William Thompson The church, Mr. Eddie Minnis painter/musician, and all around good Bahamians and icons, Mr. Lou Adams musical Icon, Mr. Avard Moncur Sports, Mr. Frederick R. Sturrup Journalist/ broadcasting, The golden girls Pauline Davis Thompson, Chandra Sturrup, Debbie Ferguson, Savatheda Fynes, Olympic gold medal winners, Mr. Duke Errol Strachan musician, Blind Blake Alphonso Higgs musician, Mr. Garnet Levarity long and noble career in government, Mr. Frank Rutherford sports, Mr. Wendell K. Jones Journalist and broadcaster, Mr. Chris Brown Sports, Dr. Cecil Bethel medical field, Ms. Tonique William Darling sports, Mr. Felix "Sonny" Johnson musician, Hon Godfrey K. Kelly Education, Mr. Thomas Augustus Robinson sports, Bishop Brice H. Thompson The church, Dame Doris Johnson women suffrage movement, Mr. Winton Gus Cooper Junkanoo icon, Mr. Calsey W. Johnson Broadcaster, Mrs. Janet Bostwick attorney/politician, Hon Carlton Francis Teacher/ politician, Sir Clifford Darling politician, Mr. Calvin Lockhart or Bert Cooper actor, Mrs. Beryl Hanna women suffrage movement, Ms. Rebecca "Becky" Chipman performer, Mr. Mark Knowles sports, Mr. Charles Carter Broadcasting Icon, Hon Paul Adderley lawyer/ politician, Mr. Edward P. St. George lawyer part owner of the port authority, Mr. Amos Ferguson artist/Icon, Mr. Brent Malone, artist/icon, Mr. James Smith Banker, Dr. Perry Gomez medical field, Ms. Debbie Bartlett media and business woman, Mr. Jackson Burnside artist and Junkanoo Icon, Dr. Gail Saunders sports and government, Sweet Richard Dean Junkanoo Icon, Sir Cecil Wallace Whitfield Politician, Mrs. Cynthia "Mother" Pratt sports/nurse/ Teacher/ Politician, Dr. Jackson Logan Burnside medical Icon, Mr. Tony Curry sports, Dr. Myles Munroe The church, Mr. Phil Stubbs, KB,

Funky D, Geno D, Nita, Terez Hepburn, Spank Band, Veronica Bishop, Elon Moxey, Ira Storr, these are all musical artist that the Bahamas is very proud of.

There are so many good and hard working Bahamians that are true to the Bahamas and its way of life. There are so many names that are not in this chapter and it remains to be seen and once we identity their names they need to be right on these pages. Unfortunately I don't know them all, but for those that are not mentioned, I would like to say, thank you, for your contribution and your dedication to your work and to the Bahamas and its people and our culture. Thanks to all of the persons that were mentioned in this charter, for where would the country be without you all, we love you honor and thank you for what you've done for the Bahamas and its people. You are truly great and honorable Bahamian men and women.

WORKING TOGETHER FOR A BETTER BAHAMAS

I cannot tell you why we as Bahamians don't like to work together any more. That is not the way it used to be back in the day, back in the day Bahamians would work together play together and live in peace and harmony. O boy I miss the good old days. In these days and times it seems like that is almost impossible, the only thing you can count on is for a lot of Bahamians to do is come together sit around and drink rum and sit around and talk about one another or fight and have some fun with one another. Isn't that sad and border line stupid? Don't get me wrong Bahamians having fun together is a good thing but when the rum comes into play with the bad headed people there goes the party and the fun. Why do we only do the bad things together and when it comes to the good things or for a good cause we don't want to work together?

I have a question for you? How can you do all of the stupid things together and all of the good things you just push aside or forget about? I forgot Bahamians have this way of thinking that it's about me, me, and only me, all for me. I am not trying to be condescending but this is the dumbest thing I've ever seen in my life. Here is what I mean and all of this that I am about to say divides us as Bahamians. The dark skin Bahamians talk about one another and fight to keep each other down and we have some dark skinned women and men who don't even want to date or have a relationship with a dark skinned Bahamian. To me that is the essence of stupidity, to say I don't like you at all because of the dark color of your skin. I say dear Heavenly father please forgive them for their ignorance and stupidity, for a person's skin color does not determine who they are, where they are going in their life or anything about them. What happened to getting to know a person and not pre-judging anybody because of the dark color of their skin, I guess getting to know or not prejudging a person is dead also.

Then you have some of the light skinned Bahamians who came from dark skinned Bahamians and some of them don't even want to talk or inter act with dark skinned Bahamian. I mean not even hi or hello I wouldn't even mention dating a dark skinned Bahamian because that's how bad it has gotten. If you are not light skinned they would ignore you. It's like they have a superiority complex and they think that they are entitled to everything and that's sad. Do not get me wrong I am not talking about all of the light skinned Bahamians just a lot of them; they remind me of the rude white people who don't even say hello or good morning and a lot of dark skinned Bahamians are a lot like that too; they have no respect for anyone anymore.

Imagine this, I dated a light skinned lady some time ago for about a year and we always talked about making back up so when we did finally talk about it, this is what she said to me about us getting back together, I have to stick with my people. My reaction was like "what"? Yeah I have to stick with my people now I'm thinking who are her people? Bahamians, but I am a full blooded Bahamian, so I asked her who are your people? And (she said) the light skinned people, cold and just like that, and after she said that I saw her in a completely different light. It was ignorant and a stupid thing to say and to believe, but it was funny how she let the cat out of the bag, so that's how some of the lighter skinned Bahamians see things? This is my case and point, and I hope she see and reads this for her own good.

You might say that I am jealous of the light shinned Bahamian but I ask you this, what is the name of this chapter? So if something as small as the color of a person's skin is the reason why Bahamians are divided and it is not bringing us any closer together but causing us to separate even more, then how would we be able to work together for a better Bahamas. If I do not point out these things that are keeping us divided I would be wrong. I do not care if they get mad because the truth is the truth and not a lie, only a lie would make you feel better, and for the record I am far from being jealous about something as ignorant and stupid as the color of a person's skin.

I feel the white Bahamians do not care anymore because they are used to having most of the money power and a lot of the say in the country, now it's half of the money and less to say, and you can take this however you want and to whoever you want, for this is the truth as I see it, and this is for who the cap fits.

This is what I call working together for a better Bahamas, working together is working hand in hand, foot to foot and putting our heads together to come up with a plan for the future of the Bahamas. We need a map to a destination because without a plan or a destination we are totally lost. This book is my plan and my map to a destination. Bahamians are just as good as anybody else and it does not matter if you are light skinned or dark skinned or white, God made you and you should have pride in that fact alone. We should show love, kindness and respect for one another, then that will transcend into growth, growth in the way you look at the difference in people, the country and in yourself. This is the way I think we should work together for a better Bahamas.

INTEGRITY

The word integrity is right up there with the rest of godly things. I mean a person who speaks the truth, honest and true to him or herself, this is another word that a lot of people in this country seem to forget about. It is like my people are slowly going mad and we forgot about all of the good things that our parents have taught us, things like, how to respect one another, how to share with one another and to be honest with one another. Also how to help one another and most of all how to love one another, this is the way Bahamians used to care about each other back in the day so why is it so hard for us to do in these days? Bahamians are some of the proudest set of people, and a lot of them are too proud, but does that mean they should not have any integrity? A person that has no integrity is like an empty barrel; don't look for anything good to come out of it.

It amazes me how some of us don't care about anything good we only want to listen to lies, talk about people and hate on one another and I don't see where doing these things gets them in their life. A lot of the people who we put in charge to run the county (the politicians) they don't seem to have any integrity in them so what are we to do? Pray to the King 1 Peter 5-7 says cast all your care upon him; for he cares for you, and he also says be diligent and add these things to your faith (2 peter 1: 4-11). If you know anything you would know that integrity is honesty and honesty is charity or love.

Please Bahamians don't be fooled by the noise or the people in the market; integrity is one of the best qualities that a person can have. Your character tells people a lot about you but integrity tells them even more about you. Stay focused and be of a sober mine, be vigilant; because your adversary the devil, walks about as a roaring lion, seeking whom he may devour (1 peter 5-8). I hope you see that the devil is not a lion he just wants you to think that. He can't devour you unless you let him. Jesus is the only conquering Lion of the tribe of Judah, trust me it will in every way benefit you to know the word of your God even if you don't believe in him, because God believes in you.

Integrity also means to take responsibility for your actions and what you say to and about people and what you do to them because you would not want them to do or say anything bad about you or to you. If you have said or done something wrong, saying you are sorry is right because sorry goes along way if you really mean it. Sorry is a small word that can fix the biggest of problems, like marital problems, friendship problems, relationship problems and a lot of the mistakes that are made by people. If you are a person that has integrity flowing through your veins saying you are sorry would be as easy as breathing. Try saying it and watch how better your soul will feel and it will bring comfort to the other person also.

What does integrity mean to me? It means just being honest with myself and others, honestly caring about people and wanting to see them do good and great things in their lives, caring about this country and where it is going and what would be left for our kids in the future. What does integrity mean to you as a child of God and as a Bahamian? Think about it.

MONEY

Money is the story of our lives. The love and need of money makes people do things they don't want to do like kill one other, stealing, lying, selling their bodies, selling drugs, cheating one another, robbing banks and each other and on and so forth. The love of money causes us to lose any sense of dignity, integrity, self worth and love for one aother because we want more and more of it. Some of us continue in the pursuit of money. Some or most of us just use it as a tool, but others look at money as power and want it so they can separate themselves from others and use it to control peoples minds but that was not God's reason for giving us money to use. In this chapter I will show you that money is not evil and how we should be using it, and how we should get it without losing our dignity, integrity and self-respect. Please read this with and open mind because I know money is a sensitive topic for most of us.

Let us start at the beginning in the book of Genesis 2:11-13. I am not going to tell you what it says I want you to look it up for yourself so you can see with your own eyes, but there are some words I want you to take note of. God made gold and it was good along with Bdellium and onyx stones. If gold and precious stones were evil the Lord God would have not said that it was good and given them to us to use and tell us right where to find them. Let's move on in Deuteronomy 8:1718 it says that: "the Lord thy God gives you the power to get wealth or money so that he may establish his covenant"? Back in those days gold, silver and precious stones were used as money to buy things but now money is made out of paper cloth and other materials and gold is used for a lot of different things including money. Countries payoff other countries with gold and platinum bars, I said all of that to say, that God in his infinite wisdom foresaw that we will need something to use to buy stuff with, just like he saw that we will need cars, boats, planes, and trains to get from one end of the world to the other end of the world (see Proverbs 8:12), and but can you imagine the world without money and what it would be like, people taking whatever they want and doing whatever they wanted, you don't have to agree with that but you think about it for a second, money is just as important to a person as knowing how to read because not knowing how to read will get you nowhere just like having no money.

Ecclesiastes 10:19 says, money answers all things; you and I know that this is true; ninety five percent of your problems can be fixed with money. I do not want to make it seem like money is everything because money is not everything, but you need money for or to buy everything.

I hope that I am clearing up that age old saying that money is the root of all evil because it is not, for it is the {love of } money that is the cause of all evil, not money (see 1 timothy 6:10). It is the {love of} money that cause's men and women destruction, and do you really think if money was really evil do you think the wise men would have brought gold to Jesus as a gift? No, they knew that he, Jesus would need money on earth.

Money is something you can always come by once you are willing to put in an honest day's work for it but it should not make your world go round. The love of God makes your world go around, whether you believe in him or not, because he surely believes in you. Do not let anyone make you feel like having lots of money is wrong but if you don't do any good with it that's wrong because to whom much is given much is expected. Whether you have a little or a lot, do good with what you can for it is better to lay up your riches in heaven than to trust in the riches of this world. Put your trust in the living God through his son Jesus Christ, always remember that.

You need money and I need money, in fact I need money right now as I am writing this book. It is safe to say everybody needs money but most of all the government needs money to keep the economy going round and round, which is why it is very important to pay income tax and company tax to the king or in other words the government. In Mathew 22:19-22 Jesus says, "Give to Caesar what belongs to Caesar or the government as long as it does not interfere with the honor that is due to god". What is due unto god is ten percent of your income just in case you did not know (see Exodus 30:11-16).

What Jesus said that makes it as clear as day that you should pay taxes to the government and I know you are wondering why I am pushing for income and company taxes so much, it is because most of the things that are wrong with the Bahamas and that needs to be fixed requires a lot of money. You have seen for yourself in the first charter of this book how much money that can be made by the people paying income taxes.

The funniest thing is we are all richer than we think or even know, here's why; "if we seek first the kingdom of God and his righteousness; and {all these things} shall be added unto you" (see Matthew 6:32-33). Jesus says ask for what you want in prayer and it shall be given to you with faith, (see Matthew 7:7-7:9-7:11 and the main one in 21:21-22), remember the story of King Solomon in all his glory, he asked for one main thing. I am not going to tell you, I want you to read the story for yourself but he asked for that one thing and it pleased God and God gave him not only that which he asked for, he also got riches beyond measure plus wisdom, knowledge and the good things of God and money. I said all of that to let you know how rich we are with the love of God through his son Jesus Christ and this kind of wealth can't surpass being rich with the love of god.

God knows what is good for you better than you know. With that said, let us use money for its intended purpose (to establish his covenant which he swore unto our for fathers), and to buy things with and as a means to get us where we want to be in life but not to love it because you know where your love should be going up above and to one another.

THE BAHAMAS LOTTERY

Man it would be sweet to win the Bahamas lottery! I know you are laughing but for how long will we allow the economy of the Bahamas to hang in limbo.

This reminds me of the guys that sit on the corner waiting for someone to come and do something for them or give them something. Why in the world, some of the smartest set of people in the Caribbean {Bahamians} can't seem to understand that we need things like the Bahamas lottery, numbers and income and company taxes so that the economy can become more stabilized. Do you want to know why there is so much crime like armed robbery house breaking and stealing in the country? It is because the young men don't have skills in order to get a well-paying job so that they can have a sense of self-worth. A sense of self-worth means they would be happy to get up for work in the morning. If the economy is not doing well then there are no jobs to go around, I would dare to say that 70% of the crime in Nassau alone has to do with money, some doing this for money or doing that for money or trying to take some money from someone or owe someone. If we build the economy up then build ourselves up think about where we could go and how far we could go, just by these four simple ideas that I'm purposing to you the people and the government.

Now let's define the difference between the lottery and a raffle, this is what the dictionary says the meaning of lottery is (1) the sharing out of money or prizes won by a game of chance (2) a gambling game in which a large number of tickets are sold and a drawing is held for money or prizes. So you mean to tell me that some churches and charities don't have a lottery, or is it because they call it by a different name. Some would say that it is a raffle not a lottery, ok then, let's look at what the dictionary has to say the meaning of raffle is (1) a form of lottery in which a number of persons buy chances to win a prize (2) a way of raising money by selling numbered tickets, one or more that win a prize.

See what the dictionary says about raffles, they are a form of lottery in which tickets are sold to raise money for a good purpose. That is the same thing to me but I guess there is a difference when it comes to the churches and charities. But when it comes to the Bahamas government it is a bad thing, they don't want the government to do it even though it will help the people and the government. Most of the times raffles only gives out prizes that does mean that there is some difference from a lottery but it is still a lottery, there is no difference, let get that clear.

So having a lottery in the Bahamas would raise money for the government to do a lot of good things for the country and would mean putting people back to work. I am wondering if the church leaders like this idea. So why hasn't the government planed and implemented the Bahamas lottery yet? I believe it is because some people don't know when to keep their mouth close and let the government run the country as best as possible.

The only thing I see them doing is stopping progress, do you have any idea how much good a lottery would do for the Bahamas, can you just imagine the possibilities? I know I can, and the people that are in charge need to stop listening to the people who are contradicting themselves and do what is best for the country and its people whether they like it or not because there is only one small group that runs this country and that would be the government and no other small group. I want them to show me where in the bible it says that it is okay to have a raffle but not a lottery, come on people let's just do what it takes to insure the financial foundation of the economy by implementing the Bahamas lottery and like it or not believe it or not it's in all of our best interest. And when they do make the lottery legal in the Bahamas they should remember that it should be one hundred percent owned by Bahamians.

PROGRESS

Progress is the answer and solution for a better Bahamas and its people but it is the ignorant and stupid _____ (you fill in the blink) that stops the progress of progress or stops progress at the door, any one you prefer. Sure you may not be able to see it, but it is so. Ignorance means the lack of knowledge and stupid means lack of intelligence, but let's hear what my God has to say about ignorance, (see Hosea 4:6-7).

Progress means to move forward or the progress of civilization, the civilization that we are living in; the Bahamas is not excluded from that and we should be able to progress towards a better Bahamas. Tell me why it feels like the more we take five steps ahead in the Bahamas it seems like something pulls us back ten steps? What is that all about and why is that happening so much in this country? Why can't we just keep moving forward like the other progressive countries in this world?

If you are a person that does not want the Bahamas to progress and I know you are not that type of person, do not let these two words be a part of you, ignorance and stupidity. Progress is the beginning of this book it is in the middle of this book and at the end of this book and the writer or author of this book; I Mr. Julian Pedican clearly defines progress by the grace and love of my God through his son Jesus Christ.

The answer and solutions in this book will continue to be present and constant with the change of governments and generations to come, for if progress was a mighty ship then this book would be the engines that move this ship forward.

We the Bahamas, are like a ship lost at sea and drifting with the wind without any compass and no GPS, this book is the GPS, the compass and the engines and with this book the leaders of the country can take us to a destination whether you believe that or not because the time has come and gone and it will keep coming and going. Until we implement these ideas we will stop progress cold in its tracks right here in the Bahamas but now the message is clear in this book, that progress is at hand or in the midst of us waiting to bloom like a flower. The Bahamians just need to take hold of it and embrace it and embrace change (means to make better or do better) because they are one and the same. To put the information in this book to the test I have no doubt in my mind that progress will come hereafter and rise on us like the sun and fall on us like the rain, (see Matthew 5:45). I know some of my people do not like to hear the word change but look at it this way whenever you hear the word change just think of my new meaning for the word charge (to make better or to do better). These are the things I would do if I was the leader of the country and this would be my map to a better Bahamas. Consider this book to be a part of my heart, a part of my mind and a little of my soul and my contribution to the Commonwealth of the Bahamas.

You can take the contents of this book however you want but I wrote this book from my honest point of view and I intend to be taken very seriously because we Bahamians cannot continue to be on the fence about the important things that are in this book. Many of the things that matters such as capital punishment are on the books but not being carried out. The playing of numbers in the country is illegal but number houses are opening up all over the Bahamas (and as simple as not wearing your seat belt after eight years of being on the books it's just being enforced), so do you see my point about being on the fence.

So what does progress mean to me? Progress is not standing still, it's moving forward and achieving better things and a better life or way of life, it is moving past a broken heart. Progress is moving forward and achieving the things that people say you cannot or we cannot achieve, progress is the beginning of everything good. Think about it Dr. Martin L. King Jr. was progress, Sir Lynden Pindling was progress, Ms. Rosa Parks was progress, Barack Obama is progress and I know you agree with me on that. My Bahamian people we have come too far with the independence of the Bahamas to stop now, we have too much good people, good places and good things to offer ourselves and the world to stop now.

It started with Sir Lynden Pindling now it is up to us to take it to the next level. If we stand still and do nothing we will achieve nothing and go nowhere as a country and I know some people will have a different opinion on this. You may differ with my view but it doesn't matter because this is my view on the Bahamas. I know you think I am being sentimental but I am being real. A bit sentimental because this is my Bahamas this is your Bahamas and this is going to be our kids Bahamas and I want the best for my kids my friends and my families kids.

Life is a journey and progress is the dependable vehicle that takes us on that journey. Whether you get into that vehicle or not it is up to you, I know I am in the vehicle and I am not getting out.

I encourage you to be a good person, do good things for people, and always look for the good in people, I know it's hard to see a lot of the times but the good is there.

Now that I have come to the end of this book it feels like ton has been lifted off my head, the things that I have written in this book are not to offend anyone but to paint a clear picture of what is going wrong in this country. All of the answers, solutions, thoughts and views and opinions are 99% my own so whether you agree or disagree, believe in or do not believe that we should use any of the answers and solutions found in this book that is totally up to you. Do not ever find yourself saying that we don't have a progressive and a carefully thought out map for the future of the Bahamas because this may not be a complete map for the future of the Bahamas but it is a start. It is right here in your hands as you read this book because when you know or we know better, we will do better, (a quote by Maya Angelo). Now that we know better we know how to do better.

I may have said some things two or three times but only so that it can be planted in your head and grow in your mind. People of the Bahamas, we cannot settle for less but if we have to settle let us make it the best that we can, this is the way I live my life.

Remember that we all have only one opportunity at this life and this book has become one of the best things that I have done so far in my life and I'm not going to stop anytime soon because this is the start of new and good things to come. It's like I've been born again with the knowledge that I have now and put a lot of wisdom, the love of God and faith into the mix. If you have that and you have a good life you have what it takes and that's what I want for the Bahamas, to have better, to do better, so that we can live better, and I don't think that's asking for too much ? What do you think? _____.

I know it sounds like I am preaching to you but if I have to come at you like a pastor in order to get my message of progress across to you, so be it. Take this as exactly that, a sermon; because if we are divided we will fail as a people but if we stand united we will progress with the love and grace of our God through his son Jesus Christ.

Here is my dream for the Bahamas and its people, I see such beautiful golden days where the Bahamas is at peace with herself like the days of old, and if you were

PROGRESS

to take a listen to her you would hear crowds and crowds of Bahamians gathered together enjoying themselves and each other. We cannot wait for tomorrow to see what good things are going to happen in the country. As you drive around the city and the islands you would be able to see that it is getting better and progress is here. You will see the beautiful people smiling with each other, I mean the black, the white and light skinned Bahamians just loving one other with no animosity. I am talking about days so beautiful you would take pictures and pictures just so you will never forget them. There will be more beautiful days like that to come, days so long and beautiful you would say to yourself this day is too beautiful and pretty to stay inside and I must be crazy to be inside and not enjoying this beautiful sunny day. I am thinking of days when you would have the sweetest and most peaceful sleep you have ever had. You don't mind if the kids make noise, days when the wind is blowing at the right time and the sun is high in the sky and hot but it's a good heat, days when you go and pickup your bad nieces and nephews and take them out to show them love because that is the essence of everything good in life (Love).

Days when the men are on the outside playing dominos and the women are on the inside talking about us men, or shopping at the mall, the grill is cooking and the kids are making as much noise as possible but that's ok because everybody is enjoying themselves and each other. Days so beautiful where the country is on one accord with most of the people, and you would see the prime minister out and about enjoying seeing his people and his country because he knows that he is a child of God and a true Bahamian. Days so beautiful when Andros and the rest of the Bahamas becomes developed beautifully, days so beautiful and wonderful you know that you don't want to live anywhere else in the world.

You know, I just want to lift my countrymen up out of the mud and wash them off and give them some new clothes and tell them, "let's go" and they would say go where? And I would say we are headed toward a bright future and my people would say what are you waiting on let's go. This is my vision for the Bahamas and its people, that the government and the people would be working together to create a better Bahamas and a better people. I know this is sounding a lot like a dream but dreams do come true. I love my people and I love being in this country and that's why I wrote this book to show my Bahamian people where we are going wrong and how we can fix it before it gets too late and out of control. I am not saying that I am right all the time and right about everything I'm just doing my best to help progress come this way and stay for a long time.

The Bahamas could become one the best countries in the world to live in and a true paradise by the grace of God through his son Jesus Christ. I believe in the willingness of the people and government to do the right things that need to be done but you might say, what am I thinking? Is he on drugs, but I'm thinking of a beautiful Bahamas, beautiful in every sense of the word, beautiful people, beautiful places, beautiful landscapes, beautiful buildings and a beautiful Bahamas. Yes I am high, high on the love of my God and life. So what if I'm dreaming of a utopian society I know that we are not perfect, but we can work together toward a utopian society just by doing some of these things I showed you in this book because let's face it the only thing that is perfect in this society is the love of God. We call the Bahamas a paradise but truly we are far from that but it is easy to get back on the right track we just need to have a plan and set a course to greatness so that the whole world will know that we stand firm in being an independent Bahamas and independent Bahamians.

The pilot or captain knows how to fly the plane and might know what's wrong with the plane but only the engineer knows how to fix the plane. The captain knows who he is and knows what I mean by this.

Thank you for buying and reading this book and I hope that it helped you to see things differently and more progressively, and May god continue to bless you and yours.

Mr. Julian Pedican

O Heavenly Father, I come unto You in prayer, O Lord God, to thank You for Your unconditional love for us all, and Your manifold grace and mercy through Your Son Jesus Christ our Lord and Savior, for without Your love, O Heavenly Father, we would be nothing, for You are my refuge in the times of war. For You are my strength in my times of weakness, for it is You that I put my trust in and build my faith upon. For You have blessed me with the site to see things other can't see, and thank You, O Lord God, for inspiring me to write this book and continue to watch my step, O Lord, so if I fail that You may pick me up again O Lord. Thank You for giving me Your wisdom and knowledge so that I can continue to become a better man, a good husband and father one day. Help them, O Lord God, that they may see that the contents of this book clearly. Help them, O Lord God, that they may have love peace and brotherly kindness in their heart so that they can move forward and closer to You. O Heavenly Father, bless them, O Lord God, that they want to make it better and to do better, so that they can always be an instrument of Your love through Your Son Jesus Christ. Amen.

Matthew 6:9-13: Our Father which art in heaven, hallowed by Thy name Thy kingdom come, Thy will be done in earth, as it is in heaven. And forgive us our debts, as we forgive our debtors, and lead us not into temptation, but deliver us from evil: for Thine are the kingdom, and the power and the glory, forever, Amen.

PROGRESS

Whether you believe in the contents of this book or not, this book is not to offend anyone. The true intent is to lead the horse to the water with hopes that it would drink. This is also to open the eyes and ears of Bahamians to things that need to be done for the country.

These are my ideas, my views, and my opinions. They are just as important to me as your ideas, views, and opinions are to you; therefore, you do not have to agree with me. However, please respect this book for what it is and what is meant for: to get the Bahamian people on one accord in getting what they want for the Bahamas and to help the Bahamas and its people to move forward and be more progressive.

Bless are you for we all have been blessed through our Lord and Savior, Jesus Christ.

Live good, be good, and do good!

Thank you.

www.ingramcontent.com/pod-product-compliance
Lightning Source LLC
Chambersburg PA
CBHW032014170526
45157CB00002B/699